the
KNOWING

the

KNOWING

*Eleven Lessons to Understand
the Quiet Urges of Your Soul*

Saje Dyer &
Serena Dyer Pisoni

sounds true
BOULDER, COLORADO

Sounds True
Boulder, CO 80306

Published 2021

Book design by Meredith March

"In a Treehouse" from *The Subject Tonight Is Love: 60 Wild and Sweet Poems
of Hafiz* by Daniel Ladinsky. Copyright © 1996 and 2003 Daniel Ladinsky,
and used with permission.

The wood used to produce this book is from Forest
Stewardship Council (FSC) certified forests, recycled
materials, or controlled wood.

Printed in the United States of America

Library of Congress Cataloging-in-Publication Data

Names: Dyer, Saje, author. | Dyer, Serena (Serena J.)
Title: The knowing : 11 lessons to understand the quiet urges of your soul
    / Saje Dyer, Serena Dyer Pisoni.
Description: Boulder, CO : Sounds True, [2021]
Identifiers: LCCN 2020038219 (print) | LCCN 2020038220 (ebook) |
    ISBN 9781683647171 (hardback) | ISBN 9781683647188 (ebook)
Subjects: LCSH: Self-actualization (Psychology) | Spirituality. |
    Forgiveness. | Conduct of life.
Classification: LCC BF637.S4 D886 2021 (print) | LCC BF637.S4 (ebook) |
    DDC 158.1–dc23
LC record available at https://lccn.loc.gov/2020038219
LC ebook record available at https://lccn.loc.gov/2020038220

10 9 8 7 6 5 4 3 2 1

To Mom and Dad. Without you, none of this is possible. Everything we have and everything we are is thanks to both of you. Beyond heaven and earth.

Serena and Saje

To Matt, Mason, Sailor, Windsor, and Forrest. I know you, and love you, by heart.

Serena

To Anthony and Julian. You are the greatest love I have known.

Saje

"Somewhere, buried deep within each of us, is a call to purpose. It's not always rational, not always clearly delineated, and sometimes even seemingly absurd, *but the knowing is there*. There's a silent something within that intends you to express yourself. That something is your soul telling you to listen and connect through love, kindness, and receptivity . . . "

DR. WAYNE W. DYER,
THE POWER OF INTENTION

CONTENTS

FOREWORD

My Knowing began as a very young girl of five when my mother brought my baby brother home from the hospital. As I held my brother, Glenn, I was thrilled by my mother's assurance that she could feel I would be a wonderful mother one day. My dream way back then was to become mother to a dozen children. Today, I'm lucky enough that seven children came through me and chose me as their mother.

From the age of twelve, I was a meditator and, having been baptized, I also understood the power of prayer. I would kneel beside my bed and say my prayer "love list" followed by a blissful silence. This bliss of existence swept over me until I woke up, as each of us does, from sleep. I had this Knowing that these minutes of silence, which I craved daily, were developing my sense of peace and Knowing that endures today.

Serena and Saje, along with the other six children in our blended family, were raised with the awareness of our inner voice and sense of Knowing—to honor that which cannot be seen or proven but which feels strangely loud and needing to be heard.

Here's an example: In 2003, when my daughter Sommer was a college student in Alabama, I received a call from the hospital that she had an open ankle fracture and needed immediate internal fixation. This surgery was to take place within the hour. Sommer and I spoke, and she was upset but already learning to accept the inevitable. We promised to talk again once she was out of surgery. I also spoke to the orthopedic surgeon, who assured me Sommer's surgery would be standard for this injury. After surgery, this doctor called and told me Sommer did fine and all went as planned. She would need a wheelchair for several weeks and then physical therapy. I felt only gratitude in knowing that such an injury caused from a simple fall was already repaired.

Once Sommer was in her hospital room, she called me and she sounded weak but also relieved that the surgery was over. She gave me the number to the phone on her bed stand. We made plans to speak each hour.

When I called again, she told me she was tired and yet found sleep elusive. I assured her that sleep in a hospital is often difficult. Foreign sounds and surroundings push sleep away. We hung up with her knowing I would call her soon to check on her. That call went unanswered, and I was relieved in thinking she probably fell asleep. The next hour passed with no answer. I tried repeatedly, still believing she was asleep.

Then I felt this sudden urge to reach her. It was a nonstop worrisome act of dialing her direct patient phone number. Something—a Knowing—told me to call the hospital directly. The operator listened to my frantic voice and sweetly said, "I'll give you the nurses' station on your daughter's floor. Call them for assistance." The phone was answered by Nurse Kathy. When I told her of my daughter Sommer not answering my calls, she assured me that Sommer was fine and that she was probably resting. And then she said, "Okay, Mom, let's go together to your daughter's room. I'll keep you on the phone with me. I always listen to a mother's urgent plea."

As I was thanking her, I heard her gasp, and the call ended abruptly. "Dear God, please take care of Sommer . . .," I pleaded.

It seemed like hours of pacing and worrying, but I believe it was less than thirty minutes when my phone finally rang. I answered suddenly and heard Nurse Kathy say, "First I want you to know, Mom, Sommer is okay." She then had Sommer tell me the same. Nurse Kathy then said, "As I walked into Sommer's room, I saw she was not breathing and I had to yell "code blue" immediately—words I felt were too harsh for you to hear. We had to restore her heartbeat with a defibrillator." Sommer then had the phone and said she woke up to so many people working on her. She said, "Mom, you saved my life. How did you know?"

We all have this inner voice of Knowing, often seen as our higher self, which whispers invaluable wisdom if we allow ourselves to hear it. I believe you have this Knowing too.

In this book, both Serena and Saje honor their higher self and the Knowing that they learned from me and from their father's worldwide teachings. They are now furthering their father's lifelong wisdom by sharing their own teachings and experiences with you to help you remember your own Knowing.

I couldn't be more proud of them and I know that Wayne is proud too.

MARCELENE DYER

INTRODUCTION

Returning to the Knowing

"The principal goal of parenting is to teach
children to become their own parents . . . You are
to be their guide for a while, and then, you will
enjoy watching them take off on their own."

DR. WAYNE W. DYER,
*WHAT DO YOU REALLY WANT
FOR YOUR CHILDREN?*

We had tears in our eyes, overcome with the thrill of
seeing our two infant boys meet each other for the first
time. When Forrest and Julian spontaneously locked
arms, we captured the moment in about two hundred
photographs in less than a minute. With that pure joy
came a deep sense of Knowing—all we had been through
in our lives and especially the past four years had led us to
this glorious, perfect, bittersweet moment—bittersweet
because we both wished our father could see this—the
little brother-cousins together.

Now that our dad was gone, for the first time ever,
we wanted to learn and apply what he had spent his
entire life teaching, and he was no longer here to talk

to about it. We experienced an acute sense of pain upon realizing that now that we had really challenging things happening in our lives and needed his message more than ever, he wasn't going to be here to supply it. We were suddenly aware that it was up to us. If we wanted to become committed to remembering the principles Dad taught, committed to remembering who we were inside, despite our worlds falling apart and transforming around us, we had to do it alone.

In this book, we share how the heartbreaking catalyst of our dad's death helped us awaken from what Jung termed the "morning" of our lives—focused on personal, physical, and material accomplishments—progress into the afternoon, and move toward evening as we make an inward shift of intention toward a higher spiritual understanding and connection within ourselves and with the world.

When we were children, everything was easy. As teenagers, we hit choppy waters but were able to learn to adjust the sails and keep going. The lessons our dad spent his life teaching millions of people seemed like teachings we could apply to our own obstacles, mostly because, unbeknownst to us at the time, compared to so many, our lives had been pretty easy. Learning to apply his work when it felt like life shit the bed? And having to do it without Dad a phone call away? That felt like drowning.

Each of us is born with the Knowing—the ability to connect to our divine, best self—and when we do, our lives align, things make sense, and we realize our purposes both small and enormous.

We didn't discover our Knowing; we returned to it.

Dr. Wayne Dyer was beloved by millions of fans around the world. Oprah called him the Father of Motivation, and strangers regularly stopped him on the street and openly wept as they told him how he'd transformed their lives, but to us, the youngest daughters of Wayne and Marcelene Dyer, he was the person we relied on for advice and gas money—our profound yet goofy dad. When he died suddenly in 2015, we were all blindsided by grief and felt unprepared to navigate life's challenges and conflicts without his guidance.

The experience launched us on an adventure from loss to understanding. Like anyone who finds themselves at a personal crossroads, we had the choice of being broken or transformed by the experience of our father's death. He'd always been there for us when we needed him, and we came to discover he still was, just in a different way. We recommitted to the teachings our dad raised us with, and our mom, too, learning to trust what we'd been rooted in from birth while branching higher and higher toward faith.

As we came to realize and metabolize our father's teachings with a new urgency, intimacy, and power and applied them to our lives—the ups and downs of relationships, young motherhood, family, careers, and crises—we ultimately found Dad's wisdom—the Knowing—was embedded in our DNA.

When Christian Nestell Bovee wrote, "Kindness is a language the dumb can speak and the deaf can hear and understand,"[1] he was speaking of the Knowing. When Albert Einstein said, "I believe in intuitions and inspirations. I sometimes feel that I am right. I do not know that I am,"[2] he was speaking of the Knowing. In the final volume of Baird Thomas Spalding's *Life and Teaching of the Masters of the Far East*, a series of books our dad was devouring right before he passed away, he underlined, "There is a light that lighteth every man that cometh into the world. That light is eternal, All-Powerful and Imperishable. Only that which is subject to birth is subject to death. The Light is the extension of God into man. It is not born nor can it die."[3] *That* is the Knowing.

Dad often told Saje he knew she had a big dharma or purpose to fulfill. "You're not quite ready yet; you still have a tendency to want to be right rather than kind. But I know that in ten years, you will be ready to start doing what I'm doing. Just place it in your imagination." It took our dad leaving his physical body as a catalyst for this to start to happen for both of us. Not that we feel like we can even come close to filling his shoes, but we are beginning to trust that it's possible to serve others through books and connecting with groups. We're starting to see the "how" and the path.

A few years ago, when Serena and Dad came up with the idea to write a book together, a book about how we were raised and what it was like to grow up in the Dyer household, Serena felt daunted yet thrilled. She wasn't sure she could adequately express what it was like to have him and Mom as parents in only ten chapters, but he was so encouraging, so loving. He worked with her, often saying, "Serena, you have a gift for telling stories. Just tell your stories, and it will be perfect." Serena felt his love and pride in her.

Dad and Serena agreed to name the book they wrote *Don't Die With Your Music Still in You* because for her, it was the most important lesson he taught. Dad came here with music to play, and he played it so loudly that it changed the world. One man, with some really big ideas, transformed the lives of millions of people for the better. Our dad, with his love of teaching, sharing, and story-telling, helped millions improve their circumstances. It is now our promise to Dad that we will not die with our music still in us. We carry on—it is our Knowing—and will do everything we can to further his message, as he asked each of his children to do in their own way.

This book is our song for him and for everyone, because we're all born with a Knowing—an inner com-pass, the quiet urgings of our soul that guide us as if randomly, but in truth, by the spoken whisper of God, the Universe, divine energy, whatever you want to call it. No matter how far removed we might become from heeding the guidance we were born to receive, it is still there, for every single one of us. Returning to our Knowing is only a matter of giving love, offering kind-ness, and paying attention.

We are grateful to have parents who shared things like that. We are grateful they taught all eight of their chil-dren to go within and find God. Grateful that they taught us to be open to other people's ideas and ways of living. They taught us to leave the judgment to someone else and, instead, to treat others with compassion, understanding that everyone is doing the best they can. Most impor-tant, we are grateful they taught us that even in death, we are shedding one coat and putting on another. Our dad told us he would never leave us, even when he departed this earthly realm, and we know this is true. He always reminded us that when the day came and he was gone and our hearts ached for him, we should think of him as though he is just in the next room, the very room from which we all originate and will one day return.

CHAPTER 1

What Is This Teaching Me?

"We live knowing that our true being is
deathless. This is a great comfort, as we can
leave sorrow behind and be inspired."

DR. WAYNE W. DYER,
LIVING AN INSPIRED LIFE

THE CALL

The most difficult year of our lives didn't make or break
us—it revealed us.

Serena was the one to get that first awful phone call.
It was August 30, 2015, and much of our family was
at Mom's in Boca Raton, celebrating the birthdays of
our sisters Sommer and Skye. Serena noticed that she'd
received a voicemail from Dee, our dad's friend, coauthor, and assistant on Maui, where he lived most of the
time and where our family spent summers. Dee followed
the message with a text asking Serena when she had last
talked to Dad. And then another. It was starting to feel
urgent, so in the middle of the celebration, Serena called
Dee back.

When she answered, Dee said she was standing in the hallway at the Westin Hotel in Kaanapali, where our dad had been staying while his condo was being renovated. Dee sounded frightened and anxious as she waited for the security guard to unlock Dad's door. This was weird, because Dee had a key, but for some reason, the deadbolt had been flipped (something Dad never did), and she couldn't get in.

As Serena waited for Dee to tell her they had opened the door, she knew in her heart something was wrong. Very wrong. It was like being in the climax of a movie, but the image was out of focus, the sound was blurry, and she couldn't fully grasp what was happening. Dee came on the phone to say they'd gotten the door unlocked, there was a shuffle on the other end of the line, and then she screamed, "*Wayne!* He's on the floor! He's on the floor!"

Serena didn't want to accept what came next, yet at the same time, the only thing she could do was press that phone to her ear so she could hear it and hear it and hear it, as if that would somehow force things to make sense as Dee repeated, "Oh my God, Serena . . . oh my God . . . *oh my God.*"

"Dee, do CPR!"

Serena heard Dee take a steadying breath before she said, "If you want me to do CPR, I will do it for you. But if you were seeing what I am seeing, you would understand . . . "

In that moment, Serena knew she would love Dee for the rest of her life, because she had heard Serena's pain and would have acted on her behalf to give her comfort, even though it was a lost cause.

As they figured out what was happening, our mom, Marcelene, our sisters, Stephanie, Skye, and Sommer, and our brother Shane, and everyone who was at the birthday party in the Florida house began sobbing—everyone was devastated, yet nobody was ready to accept what was unfolding. In the next instant, Serena was on the phone with a police officer.

"What is your relationship to the deceased, Ms. Dyer?" he asked.

"Who is deceased?"

"Oh, I thought you knew . . . I am sorry to tell you that this man is deceased, and we need to collect information."

Serena handed the phone to our mom. She couldn't talk while simultaneously processing that our dad, who we'd each been in touch with via text or phone or email just the day before, was no longer breathing. Serena pulled herself together enough to call Saje.

Saje had returned home to New York City two days earlier after a trip through Australia and New Zealand with our dad, Skye, and Skye's husband, Mo. She was a bit jet-lagged but nonetheless excited to be back and to start her next semester studying for a master's degree in psychology at New York University. She was sitting on the couch with Anthony (her then-boyfriend, now husband), who was engrossed in a preseason football game on TV, when the phone rang. She remembers thinking it was strange that Serena would call during the family celebration.

As soon as Saje answered the phone, she could tell something was horribly wrong. Serena's tone of voice and energy sent terror through her. Serena asked Saje if she was alone, and when she told her she was with Anthony, Serena said to sit down. Saje was confused but did as she asked. That was when Serena spoke the words that have resounded in our minds more times than we can count: "Dad doesn't have a pulse."

Saje didn't understand what Serena was saying; she panicked, screaming, "What do you mean? What do you mean? *What do you mean, he doesn't have a pulse?* Are they trying to give him a pulse? Are they giving him a pulse?" (Later, when Saje asked Serena why she had phrased it "Dad doesn't have a pulse," Serena said it was because she could not utter "Dad is dead." Those words were impossible for her to say aloud or even comprehend, and she simply couldn't bring herself to do it.)

Anthony turned off the television and rushed to Saje. At this point, she had dropped the phone and stopped speaking. She could not understand what was going on, and could no longer formulate cohesive thoughts. She was hyperventilating as the life she knew evaporated. Serena screamed through the speaker, asking, "Are you okay? Are you still there?" but Saje couldn't make her arms move to pick up the phone.

Anthony comforted Saje while simultaneously retrieving the phone. He asked Serena what was going on. At this point, Saje still thought that Dad was going to be okay; he must be in an ambulance or being resuscitated. She got ahold of herself and asked Anthony what Serena was telling him. He looked at her, tears streaming down his face, and said, "Saje, I'm so sorry. Your dad died."

It's impossible for Saje to fully convey what that moment was like. It is difficult not only because she doesn't have the language to describe what she felt but because her mind has put a sort of filter on this memory. When Anthony gave her the awful news about our dad, she blanked out. She went numb. She was in disbelief, in shock. Until then, she hadn't fully understood what it meant to be in shock. It's not a feeling that is possible to communicate to someone who hasn't experienced it. But if we were to try, it's like being given information that shatters your entire world so suddenly and profoundly that your mind attempts to reject it as a way of self-protection, and then your body becomes unreactive to your thoughts.

Saje began to gasp and sob. She kept thinking she should call our dad—something we all did regularly with news large and small, from college acceptances to a joke we knew he would like—and then she realized that she would never get to do that again. Heartbreak set in.

Serena had to call Tracy, our eldest sister, next. She was devastated, and there was complete silence on the phone until Tracy said that she needed to process this and would call Serena back. Our little brother Sands was in Nicaragua at the time, and Serena had to call him next. Realizing this made her feel like she might vomit. Sands and our dad had a father-son bond like no other. They spoke the same way, moved the same way, lived by the same philosophy. The idea of telling our brother Dad was dead was too great a burden to bear. Serena handed the phone to Mom again and watched as she fell apart, trying to find the words to tell her son.

We could hear Sands throw the phone, screaming "No! No! No!" His friend got on the line and said, "Sands took off running for the ocean." Sands jumping into the water—that's a scene we'll never be able to let go of. Our brother, after finding out that our dad wasn't alive, ran to the ocean, the thing that has given him indescribable comfort since he was a little boy, the very thing he was named for. It breaks our hearts to think about it.

After that phone call, Serena walked outside. Skye came out to join her. They looked at each other—they couldn't cry, and words seemed useless.

What followed were dozens of phone calls and texts and emails to all the people in our dad's world: Maya, our dad's other assistant of thirty years; Reid, his publisher and best friend; and our dad's two brothers, who couldn't fathom that their younger brother, so healthy and full of life, was suddenly gone from the Earth, his body on its way to the morgue.

AN ODD YET PERFECT ONENESS

The rest of that day is blurry for Saje. She wanted to know the details of what happened to our dad but could not speak. She wanted to run and break free from this insane agony but could not move. She wanted to talk to our dad, but it was no longer a possibility. She started to feel so claustrophobic in their small studio apartment that she asked Anthony if he would walk with her to the Hudson River.

Being alive felt surreal on that walk. Saje wore sunglasses, and the tears flowed from under them as, hand in hand with Anthony, she passed person after person. She felt great compassion toward these strangers because she was aware of how much she was suffering in that moment and knew that they did not know that she was suffering, which made her wonder if *they* were suffering and *she* did not know it. Looking back, it seems like an odd time to feel this kind of oneness, but it also makes perfect sense.

Once Anthony and Saje had walked the four blocks to the Hudson River and arrived at "their" bench, where they often sat and had breakfast on sunny days, Saje did a lot of reflecting, and tears fell as Anthony did his best to comfort her. Her phone started to buzz with calls, texts, and social media messages from friends, loved ones, and strangers around the globe. She decided to turn the alerts off, to suspend all contact with the outside world, and to see Dad in the waterbirds flying above, in the wind blowing her long hair off her face, and in the river flowing with such quiet force. For the first time since Serena had called, Saje experienced a sense of calm.

Our dad used to love to quote a line from *A Course in Miracles*—the classic text of spiritual transformation that influenced so much of his teaching: "I could see peace instead of this."[1] Saje did not feel in a state to even have meaningful or logical thoughts, yet up popped this remarkable advice that offered immediate relief . . . *she could see peace.*

Although it was brief, it was significant. She had touched the Knowing—her elemental divine self—something we would both learn to look to for guidance and comfort during the turmoil that overtook us during the hours, days, and months of grief that followed. Saje might have believed that the idea of being able to be peaceful in the worst moments of her life came out of nowhere, but that's not so. You see, these kinds of thoughts are not always random, nor are they necessarily our own thoughts. It's up to us to tune in and listen.

Connecting to that moment of stillness, of peace, helped Saje move forward with the practicalities of the next few days. Her first step was to join our family in Florida as soon as possible. While Anthony booked their flight out for the following morning, our brother Sands called her. When she saw his name on the buzzing phone, her soul lurched. She wanted nothing more than to speak to the person who is most like our dad on the planet. In some illogical way, it felt like our dad was calling. On the other hand, her heart broke into even more pieces as she realized the agony Sands was in at that moment.

She answered, and they both sat in silence—a silence that was full of understanding. Here was a person who completely understood what she felt, just as she understood what he felt. In that moment, a wave of gratitude washed over Saje as she realized how fortunate she was to have not only Sands, who could completely understand what she was going through, but six more siblings—Serena, Shane, Skye, Sommer, Stephanie, and Tracy—plus our mom to console and heal with. Many people in the world lose someone and are alone. We knew we would never be abandoned in our sorrow, which was another reason to see peace and have gratitude on that sad day.

Eventually Sands and Saje spoke, and although the conversation was one of tears and shock, dismay and despondency, there was also laughter and pure love for our father, a mutual Knowing that this was his time to go, as they reflected on the ways they knew for sure everything was perfect. Because Saje had been traveling with Dad for the past three weeks, Sands asked her a lot of questions about what he was like during the trip to Australia and New Zealand. He wondered whether Dad had seemed tired or less like himself or if there was any other sign that those would be his final weeks in his physical body. Saje told Sands that they had had an amazing trip, full of laughter and making memories. Based on Dad's physical health and state of mind, she'd had no warning that those were to be his last weeks.

Later, as his death launched a series of events in our lives both practical and spiritual, worldly and transcendent, we all came to believe that Dad might have known what was going to happen all along.

LINES OF COMMUNICATION

When Serena finally drove home that night, she got into bed but couldn't sleep. She lay there, trying to talk to our dad and say what she might have said to him during a normal phone conversation the day before. Eventually, she arrived at a place of Knowing that she was in one of the most profound events of her life—right in the center of it—yet couldn't process her immense fear of eternity, of forever. Everyone who knows Serena knows she is a talker. Our dad was a talker too—her conversations with him were her favorite things in the world. That was the hardest part for her about all of this. Their relationship was built on talking to each other. They spoke on the phone almost every single day. Like all our siblings, Serena called Dad first whenever anything important happened. Even when her water broke in the middle of the night as she went into labor with her daughter, Sailor, she called him before anyone else despite the fact that she was in Florida and he was in Maui.

This time, she tried but felt fake talking to him. It was not at all like speaking with Dad on the phone or in person; instead, it seemed vacant and empty. She knew from the things he'd said while he was alive that continuing to speak to him, to connect with him, even in her mind was important, no matter how weird or uncomfortable, so she continued to try, eventually asking for a sign. Dad had been talking about when he would die and what the "other" side was like for as long as we could all remember. His "next adventure" was a regular topic of conversation at the family dinner table, and we often discussed how he would communicate after he passed away.

When Dad's mother (our grandmother) died, he received some of her ashes, and we'll never forget how, while touching those ashes, he repeated these opening lines from an Emily Dickinson poem[2] from memory:

> This quiet Dust was Gentlemen and Ladies,
> And Lads and Girls;

He went on to tell us, "Surely my mother, who was once a girl with curls, a lady, a friend, and so much more, surely she is not just quiet dust. I can feel her now with me as I say this. The soul is not limited to the physical body; it transcends this temporary limitation and lives on."

While Serena recalled these memories about our dad, she felt an odd urge to listen to his weekly podcast. She had never listened to his or anyone's podcast before. She didn't even know there was a podcast app on her phone, but she was drawn to the idea and clicked the button, typed in "Wayne Dyer," and pushed play on the first episode that came up.

The podcast was adapted from his radio show. Callers asked him questions or discussed things that mattered to them, and Dad had provided them with comfort or calming wisdom. As she listened, his voice soothed her, and she relaxed, all the while thinking that it was great to hear his voice, but this wasn't exactly the type of sign she had been hoping for. Then, at the end of this randomly chosen podcast, he said: "And now I want to take a moment for my daughter Serena, who is going through a hard time, so if we could all send her love, that would be great."

Serena bawled her eyes out! She had never cried so hard in her life. It was a shock to hear him mention her name and ask his audience to send love. She eventually stopped crying and said out loud, "Okay, Dad. I get it. You are still here, but I can't believe you pulled it off. I seriously can't believe you actually died and pulled it off."

It seems weird that the words that kept running through her mind were "pulled it off." She still couldn't grasp that after an entire lifetime of hearing our dad talk about how he genuinely looked forward to the next adventure, he was now embarking on it. She decided she would do her best not to remain stuck in the grief, fear, or lingering sorrow losing a loved one causes. She would remain open to learning to see and hear Dad but in a new and distinct way. This was, like many things in life, harder than she thought it would be.

TRUSTING THE PERFECTION

That night, before her early-morning flight to Florida, sleep eluded Saje as well. After a few hours of intermittent sobbing, she decided to turn on her laptop. She did not know what came over her, but she had a burning desire to write.

> Today I lost the most important man in my life—my father. To so many people in the world, he was a great teacher and a person of infinite wisdom. Although he was these things for me, even more so, he was always my dad. He was the person I turned to whenever I had an issue. He was the person who I always called first when I had good news. Every time I got an A on a paper, I immediately sent it to him, and he would praise my work and make me feel talented.

> My dad was never the type to tell me what to do. Even when I asked, he would respond, "Saje, I cannot tell you what is right for you, only you know that. It wouldn't be right for me to impose my desires on you." As I have gotten older, I have started to realize that my father's way of parenting was not the norm. I am infinitely grateful for the wisdom he allowed me to gain by insisting I choose my life—because even though at times I may have chosen wrong, the lessons I learned were my lessons and no one else's.

> I cannot truly comprehend he is gone. I am filled with images of him lifeless and of what his last moments would have been like. My heart

aches in a way that I did not know it could. Tears flow as I'm filled with the greatest sense of loss I have ever experienced. Amid all this chaos and turmoil, I am reminded of so many of the truths my dad gave to me and to the world.

I was blessed to have spent the last three weeks traveling throughout Australia and New Zealand with Dad, Skye, and Mo. We shared so many laughs and we all grew even closer. During our five days in Australia and New Zealand, I listened to Dad speak and lecture to many gatherings. On countless occasions he talked about the beauty of death, how he envied those who have passed on to the infinite world of love. He spoke about the new book he co-authored with Dee—*Memories of Heaven*—stories of children recalling their experience of heaven before they incarnated into their bodies on this earthly plane. He also shared his belief that whenever we are confronted with the death of a loved one, we have the choice to get over our sadness "sooner or later," and said, "I always tell people and myself to choose sooner."

The entire experience shifted my perception of death, so tonight, despite this great chaos and turmoil that my mind insists I experience, I am reminded of so many ideas my dad taught, like that we are not our bodies, nor are we our minds. There is a part of us that is infinite and that is pure love, and that is who we truly are. While I am still a person with a body and a mind, I am not able to abandon the deepest sadness that I have ever felt in my life. However, when I get still and am able to hold my sobs back for a moment or two, I am comforted in an unexplainable way because I know that my dad is now part of this infinite world that he so ardently studied and taught about.

Writing this is the calmest I have felt since I got the news earlier today that my dad no longer had a pulse. I will miss my father for so many endless reasons—but Dad, I know that you are with me now, and forever. I love you more than I feel I can explain, and I am forever grateful for the wisdom, the laughs, and all the memories that you have given me. I love you forever.

Remembering these things, Saje connected to being still and her Knowing that Dad was with us forever and we could trust that everything is perfect. It confirmed that he was already comforting us and guiding us from the other side. It proved we were stronger than we thought. We'd need that strength in the days ahead, because our lives were going to get a whole lot harder before they got easier.

THE QUESTIONS THAT BRING PEACE

Even in these early, heartbreaking days, we inherently knew we had to allow our perspective to shift from overwhelming sorrow and longing to asking, "What is this teaching us?" We began to take our first steps toward experiencing miracles and wisdom, entering the Knowing.

Not wondering, "Why us?" but "How we can use what we learned from both of our parents—our father, who has passed on, and our mother, who is still with us—to serve our loved ones and our own deepest calling even during the most difficult times?"

Throughout our lives, our dad often quoted the psychologist Carl Jung, who wrote, "Thoroughly unprepared, we take the step into the afternoon of life; worse still, we take this step with the false assumption that our truths and ideals will serve us as hitherto. But we cannot live the afternoon of life according to the program of life's morning; for what was great in the morning will be little at evening, and what in the morning was true, will at evening have become a lie."[3]

We were gradually waking up to the afternoon of our lives. At first, we believed we were thoroughly unprepared to deal with the grief of losing our dad but also to navigate all the difficulties and conflicts that arose in our personal lives after his passing.

Who would walk Saje down the aisle when she got married? Who would give her a sense of worth and accomplishment every time she achieved anything, from making a vegetable soup to writing a term paper? Who would throw her future children in the air as they squealed with glee and tickle them silly? Who would she phone to discuss anything from life's biggest questions to that day's small news?

How would Serena ever teach her young daughter how incredible her grandfather truly was? How would she pass Dad's wisdom to her growing family without him to gently remind her when she slipped? How would she make it through this difficult time in her life without his daily (sometimes hourly) words of wisdom and support? How would she mirror his unconditional love to her own children without his presence?

As we learned to connect to our Knowing, we sought and united with a higher spiritual understanding of the unfolding of events in our lives and realized that—like Dorothy and her ruby slippers in *The Wizard of Oz*—we had the tools to enter this new experience. This truth was within us all along. The roots of our Knowing reached back to the moment we were conceived. Our parents, who would never tell us what to do and insisted we knew what was right for ourselves, had been training us for exercising our Knowing for our whole lives.

When discussing "God," our family saw the term as interchangeable with *universe* or *spirit*. We firmly believe that "it" doesn't care about a name. As the poet Rumi famously wrote, "What was said to the rose that made it open, was said to me in my heart, when I met You." Rumi was speaking of meeting God, all the while never doubting the Knowing that resided within him and that he only had to "polish the mirror" to see God's face.

Seven centuries later, in *Man's Search for Meaning*, Holocaust survivor and psychologist Victor Frankl wrote, "We must never forget that we may also find meaning in life even when confronted with a hopeless situation, when facing a fate that cannot be changed. For what then matters is to bear witness to the uniquely human potential at its best, which is to transform a personal tragedy into a triumph, to turn one's predicament into a human achievement. When we are no longer able to change a situation—just think of an incurable disease such as an inoperable cancer—we are challenged to change ourselves."[4]

This wisdom evolved into our dad's most famous line: "When you change the way you look at things, the things you look at change." When we lost our dad, we faced a fate that could not be changed. Because we could not change the situation, we had to challenge our experience of profound loss and devastation and staying stuck in that grief into something that could help us to grow. Dad left at just the right time just as he was born at just the right time, just like we all are. Allowing yourself to shift your perspective allows you to connect with so much more, especially the Knowing.

Go within and ask yourself what it is that you want. What are you trying to do? Is it something that fulfills the ego or is of service? You'll arrive at your highest self when the answers to these questions bring peace—not what your ego wants. The ultimate peace you can arrive at is to feel God within yourself, and that is your Knowing.

A Way of Knowing

When you *challenge* the way you look at things, the things you look at change.

That first year after Dad died was so difficult because we were finally coming to know ourselves and to reevaluate our identities without his support and mirroring. We felt like we had to find our way home in the dark—until we realized he was there all along. Anyone who knows our dad's work is familiar with one of his most famous sayings: *When you change the way you look at things, the things you look at change.* We've found this starts with bringing your awareness to each situation you are in—the Knowing that personal tragedies can always be turned into triumphs and opportunities to grow.

When you find yourself in situations that are outside your control, we've found the best thing you can do is ask, "What is this here to teach me?" as opposed to saying something along the lines of "Why me?" Another line we heard frequently from our dad was, "You're only stuck if you choose to be."

When Saje was in her early twenties and struggling through her first real heartbreak, she was sitting at the dinner table with Dad, barely holding it together. As she pushed the food around her plate, he asked her if she was okay. She began to let it all out, and he realized how much she was hurting in that moment. Dad spoke some words that Saje has carried with her ever since. He explained that life is often like a wave. When we are riding the crest, it is exhilarating, and we can find ourselves feeling almost invincible. But then we make our way down to the trough, and compared to the crest, life can just feel difficult, almost impossible. The key is to realize that the troughs are just as important as the crests and often have the most to teach us. The troughs provide us with the opportunity to truly challenge and change the way we are looking at life and thus to grow as people and watch as the things we are looking at evolve before our eyes. Even more important: we are never stuck unless we choose to be. Bringing this wisdom into Saje's heartbreak allowed for the healing to settle in, and it was a catalyst for the life she now lives and for which she is eternally grateful. As the saying goes, "No storm lasts forever."

When we made the conscious decision to shift and choose to see Dad's passing not only as an opportunity to get to know him from the other side but also as an opportunity to become more compassionate and selfless people, the whole situation changed before our very eyes.

If you change the way you look at things, the things you look at change . . . Although this might sound like just a clever little play on words, the reality behind this maxim is found in the field of quantum physics, which has proven that at the subatomic level, the act of observing a particle changes the way the particle acts; the energy of the person viewing the particle actually changes the particle itself! In other words, the way in which we observe these particles can determine what they ultimately become. Everything that makes up the physical world can be broken down into particles and then subatomic particles, including the human body. So it is not a stretch to believe that when we change how we look at a situation, the situation will quite literally change. This is the same as the simple truth that until you are ready to receive a lesson, it doesn't matter how many times you hear that lesson in a thousand different ways. You must be in alignment with what the lesson is trying to teach you in order for the message to stick. The energy that you bring to each situation you find yourself in determines the outcome you ultimately experience.

Applying this to death or anything that feels hopeless, insurmountable, or tragic works elegantly. Making this shift in perspective makes way for miracles (which are the opposite of accidents). Although we can view death as accidental, surely there is something greater than us moving the pieces on the chessboard that is our life. However, we must surrender to that Knowing and trust that it is all in divine, perfect, order. We cannot always see the "why," but we can choose to believe that something bigger than us *can*.

At some point in life, everyone experiences profound loss, and most of us experience it again and again, because death is simply a part of life. Grief is all-encompassing, and when you're in it, it's blinding. It can feel like it will never end. Joy can feel so out of reach that you can't even relate to the concept of it any longer. So is there anything that you can even do when you find yourself in this pervasive type of grief? Take a deep breath. What you are feeling is real and it is profound and it is important, but it does not last forever. Remind yourself of this when it starts to feel hopeless by saying, "What I am feeling now is real, but I will not always feel the way I do now." For us, saying these simple words can instill some hope, and hope is really all you can ask for in those early days. Unfortunately there is no magic pill that can take your pain away. But by instilling some hope, you will open yourself up to the miracles that your loved ones who have passed on are waiting to share with you. Repeat the words from *A Course in Miracles* that have brought us so much comfort in those moments when it felt hopeless: "If you knew who walks beside you on the way that you have chosen, fear would be impossible."[5] Seek that place of *knowing* that your loved ones are beside you and say these words until you really feel it. Every single person who has lived on this planet has either already passed on or will pass on. So where have they all gone? They are here with us, simply in another form. Contemplating this idea has always brought us comfort, and our sincere hope is that it can do the same for you as well. It challenges the jarring notion that not only are our loved ones gone forever, but their death was some sort of accident or tragedy, when in reality everything happens according to divine timing.

When we give up our own ideas of the way things should have or could have been and instead adopt complete faith that it was the way it had to be, we experience the miraculous guidance that has been available to us all along. That's why, for us, the lesson has evolved into "When you *challenge* the way you look at things, the things you look at change," because when our dad died, we were challenged to change the way we looked at his death—not as tragedy but as divine timing—and this changed the experience of receiving his guidance and signs and ultimately reconnected us with our own inner Knowing.

CHAPTER 2

Parented in Pure Love

"The purpose of dancing—and of life—is to
enjoy every moment and every step, regardless
of where we are when the music ends."

DR. WAYNE W. DYER,
LIVING AN INSPIRED LIFE

ONE SIMPLE RULE

During the private celebration of Dad's life in Boca
Raton, Florida, our childhood babysitter, Kelly, shared
her memories of our father. She reflected on the day in
the late 1980s when she responded to an ad in the Help
Wanted section of the local Boca Raton newspaper for
part-time childcare. Kelly was excited to set up an interview with our mom. At this point, our parents had six
kids, with the three youngest ranging in ages from one
to five, Sands on his way, and Saje still to come in a year
or so—clearly, our mom needed some help! Our mom fell
in love with Kelly and hired her on the spot. As she told
this story at the memorial, she recalled a poignant moment
during her first day that let her know that our family was

a little out of the ordinary but in a way that resonated with her. On the day our dad first met Kelly, he explained to her that as our babysitter, she was going to have an important role in raising and shaping his kids, and he asked her to follow one simple rule: "Teach only love."

He meant it. We were never told who to marry, what type of religious beliefs to have, what clothes to wear, or who to vote for as we got older. We were influenced by our parents' ways of being and thinking, but they refused to label us, refused to tell us what to do with our lives, relationships, or careers. Because of that, we were raised on a type of love that taught "I love you for who *you* are, with no requirement that you do anything or be anyone to satisfy *me*. I love you unconditionally, and because of that, I place no expectations or requirements on who you ought to become. Be you and no one else. That is all I ask of you as your mom and dad." Our parents were so committed to this type of love, to this type of energy in our home, that they even had a bumper sticker on our minivan that said: "I am a proud parent . . . unconditionally!" We can't tell you the number of times other parents honked at us as we drove by and gave a big, goofy thumbs-up.

During our dad's celebration of life, Kelly accurately pointed to the essence of how our parents raised us. There weren't strict bedtimes, and we didn't have to sit at the table until our veggies were finished; there was simply an atmosphere of love and support combined with an expectation to be loving and supportive. Our parents led by example and allowed us to find our own ways to tap into the moral compass that each of us is born with, what we like to call our own inner Knowing.

GROWING UP DYER

People often ask us what our childhoods were like, and although it seemed normal at the time, we've come to realize that our upbringing was something truly special. The love we felt growing up was so pure it is almost as if we have an innate desire to protect it, to keep it private, and, in doing so, keep it sacred. Neither one of us realized how wonderful this dynamic was for us, especially the youngest five of us, until we were older.

In our family there are eight children. Tracy is the oldest. Then Shane and Stephanie. The youngest five of us—Skye, Sommer, Serena, Sands, and Saje—were all born within an eight-year timespan, so to say we are close is an understatement. We shared rooms as kids. We all went to the same school and had the same friends. For years, some of us chose to not only share a room but also share a bed so we could hold hands and tell stories at night. Like all children, we fought—trust us, we had fights!—but falling out of favor with the pack was worse than being in trouble with our parents, so we learned to resolve our bickering so we could go back to having fun. We also learned to resolve our differences, because our parents did not get involved when we were arguing over a toy or whose turn it was or whatever ridiculous fight we as children engaged in. Our parents always told us to work it out, and because we were not getting their attention by fighting, we fought less than we might have had they always come running to solve our petty issues. Our mom, an incredibly strong and quiet woman, was content with taking the back seat to our dad and his consuming career, often being left alone for long periods of time with us children so that our dad could travel, speak, and write.

According to Saje,

> Mom was almost always calm. When I think of my childhood with her, I think of a serene and loving presence constantly with me, giving me the space to be myself, while simultaneously never being so separate that I didn't feel her loving guidance. Our Mom has never taken life too seriously. I can remember a time when Sands was getting into trouble in school because when he was with certain friends, he would break into uncontrollable laughter, and it would serve as a distraction in class. When Mom was asked to come in to meet with the principal and the teacher as well as Sands, she and Sands broke into a contagious laughing fit during their discussion about the uncontrollable laughter! The principal and teacher ended up joining in that day, and the issue was resolved by giving Sands some tools to help him keep his laughter to the playground and lunchtime.

We grew up in Boca Raton, Florida, and spent our summers on Maui. We all shared a two-bedroom condo, and the youngest five of us, plus a friend or two, would somehow figure out how to put a cot in between the two twin beds and make one giant bed spanning the length of the bedroom, where we all slept for June, July, and August every summer, at least until Sands was old enough to realize he was the only boy in the room and opted for the couch.

We always knew our parents were a little different. Unlike most fathers, our dad went to "work" every day in tennis shorts, a T-shirt (usually a free shirt he received from a stranger in the mail), and Birkenstocks. It was common for our parents' friends, who were monks, psychics, mediums, healers, and spiritual enthusiasts, to come over for dinner in Boca or Maui, and no topic of conversation was ever off limits.

Every summer on Maui, we would pile into the minivan and drive more than an hour to visit our family friends Frederick and his sister Meenakshi. Fredrick was a Buddhist monk who lived in the middle of the rainforest completely off the grid in a building on stilts that he built himself over many years. This one-room home, with majestic views of the ocean, was the gathering place for our annual lunch, followed by a meditation that always turned into a laughing fit. Frederick would prepare a completely vegan meal, usually containing mung beans, and as kids, we would do everything we could to move the food around our plates so it appeared we had eaten, often trying to sneak it onto someone else's plate when they weren't looking. After we'd pretended to eat, Frederick would suggest we sit in a circle and chant, and no matter how hard we tried, none of us could suppress our laughter. Once someone's stifled laughter was heard, we would all erupt into hysterics, usually led by our mom, who can never keep a straight face in situations in which a straight face might be expected. Always a good sport, Frederick joined in, saying that laughter was, in itself, a pure form of meditation.

It never occurred to us growing up that people *didn't* meditate. For as long as we could remember, there was a sign on our parents' bedroom door that read "Mom is meditating for TWENTY MINUTES . . . please do not disturb!" and we knew that unless someone was bleeding or throwing up, we should not disturb her meditation. What was good for Mom and Dad was good for us kids too, and they taught us Transcendental Meditation when some of us were still in elementary school.

FREEDOM FROM GUILT

When we were young children, our mom did everything for us. She was the constant caregiver, the bandager of wounds, the preparer of meals. She was the one who bathed us, who came to all our school functions; she was the ever-present nurturer. Our dad was focused on his writing, his teaching, and his work, but our mom's attention was solely on her family. That is why, to this day, every single one of her children calls her every day, and most of us get together with her multiple times a week.

As much as our mom was the nurturer, our dad was the playful one. Both of our parents had a reverence for children, particularly babies, and Serena distinctly remembers, after giving birth to her daughter Sailor, how Dad told her that her child contained all the wisdom of the universe. He said that Sailor was born with her own soul, her own sense of being, and Serena's only job as a mom was to guide and then step aside. He told her that she needed to honor who her child was, whoever that might be, without ever trampling on the delicacy of her spirit by imposing on her who Serena *thought* she should be or what Serena thought her daughter ought to do with her life.

Mom and Dad made it a point to celebrate children and their Godliness. They appreciated how children are always in the moment, in awe of their surroundings, and view everyone they meet as a friend, as a new person to love—this was our parents' mutual Knowing. Our dad used to say, "Watch a child's excitement when they see a rainbow and remember that space within you that once felt that same excitement over a rainbow . . . or a balloon, or the simplest of things. Stay in the space of awe, of joy, over everything." Now that we both have small children, it is easy for us to remember our own thrill over something as simple as a flower or the moon, because our children are constantly in that space of awe. Watching them has helped us remember our own childlike awe, and more and more, we choose to come from that space. As Rumi wrote, "Sell your cleverness and buy bewilderment."

Because of our parents, as children we could completely be ourselves and always felt that our voices were heard and that who we were was being honored. Saje was a tomboy as a child and preferred to wear basketball shorts and big T-shirts until she was about ten, and this was completely fine. When our sister Skye was in her final year of college, she decided she wanted to take a break from school and pursue her calling of being a singer, to which our parents responded with love and support. They felt that she, at the age of twenty-two or so, was certainly capable of making a decision like this about her own life, and they were not about to force her to complete something just for the sake of receiving a piece of paper that said she had completed it. They allowed her to choose the trajectory of her life by encouraging her to tap into her own Knowing. When Serena decided to go to college at Arizona State University, there was no pressure from either parent that she be closer to home or pursue a particular field of study. When Serena insisted she attend cotillion to learn "proper dinner-table etiquette," something our parents were never concerned about, they happily drove her to each class and even attended the ball upon her completing the course, even though dad came in his Birkenstocks while the other fathers wore tuxedos!

For the first few years of elementary school, Saje attended a Lutheran school. In second grade, she started coming home upset, because hanging in the chapel at this school was a giant cross and a hyperrealistic portrayal of Jesus's crucifixion, with nails piercing his wrists and blood all around the nails. The teachers explained that Jesus was paying for all the sins of humanity, but even when she was a small child, this notion didn't sit right with her. Saje was so upset that after some consideration, our parents decided to allow any of their children who desired to leave this Lutheran school to attend a local secular school instead. Serena, who was older and had established friendships, decided to stay at the Lutheran school, whereas Saje opted for the new one. Even when she was in the second grade, our parents honored who Saje was. Serena and Saje can reflect and recognize what an invaluable gift their parents have given them by loving them for exactly who they are.

As we got older, we became aware of how our friends' parents used guilt to motivate their kids to do what they wanted, saying things like, "You're going to go out and leave me to have dinner by myself?" or "If you don't come home for Christmas, who will I spend the day with?" We're not saying it's a terrible thing to do, but it does create a situation in which kids are acting out of guilt and not their own desires. This is something our mom and dad never did—they never parented with guilt. If we said we were going to be with them, that was great, and if we said we had other plans, that was also fine. What we've come to understand from this method of parenting is that we and our siblings constantly wanted to be around our mom (and our dad when he was alive), possibly even more than they wanted us to be! Perhaps this was because of the simple truth that when you don't feel fenced in by your parents or loved ones, you are more drawn to them. When you take away expectations and pressure from any relationship, you create the space for love to flourish, and what child wouldn't be drawn to that?

ENTHUSIASM

The most striking thing about those early years, though, is that our parents were individually committed to following their dreams, their dharmas. *Dharma* was a word we heard often. It is a Sanskrit term that has a range of translations and definitions, but in our family, it meant "your life's purpose, your passion, your calling."

Our mom felt strongly that her dharma was to become a mother. She had seven natural childbirths and then began coaching other women in doing the same. She often told us this was her purpose, her calling, and she gave herself wholeheartedly to it. To this day, we don't know that we have ever seen a woman as devoted to her children and fifteen (so far . . .) grandchildren as our mom. It isn't just that when we were children, she met all our needs and made sure each of us was given the opportunity to attend the new activity we were interested in or go out for the sport team we wanted to join. Beyond the daily task of parenting, our mom made sure that each of us knew we were loved and supported no matter what. She raised us to *experience* love, not just be told that we are loved. She never seemed tired of us, she never seemed overwhelmed by us, and she made it clear that although our dad was following his dharma on a global scale, she was also following hers in our home. Mother Teresa is often quoted as having said, "If you want to change the world, go home and love your family." Our mom did this daily . . . hourly. She understood the importance of giving her children the solid foundation they needed to be good people in the world before and after they left the nest, and she understood that it was her soul's purpose to do so.

Our dad was also committed to following his passion and the things in life that called to his soul, and he made sure that we understood that in order for him to do that—to teach and lecture on a global scale—he often had to miss one of our soccer games or school plays. He didn't become one of the bestselling authors of all time and a life counselor and spiritual guide to millions of people by staying at home. He traveled a lot, but there was never a time, not even once, when we were disappointed that he could not attend something of ours. That might be difficult to believe, and it is worth pointing out that our dad did a great job of making sure he was there for anything important, but there were times he had to miss things, and the feeling we kids shared was one of pride in him, pride that he was so devoted to his work, to his mission of bringing light to the world, of bringing peace and hope where there was suffering. We never expected him to skip that in order to see our seventeenth basketball game of the season.

Our dad was so dedicated to following his dreams, to honoring what excited his soul, that seeing him pursue this gave each of us, on a subconscious level, permission to do the same. He was not telling us to follow our dreams while simultaneously giving up his own. He lived in such a way that he was constantly *demonstrating* what it looked like to follow your dreams. He showed us, his children, that honoring what you feel called to do will require work and sacrifice, but there is no greater feeling in the world than knowing you are doing the work of your highest self, the work that the God within you is calling you to do. We often heard our dad explain that *enthusiasm*, when traced back to the Greek that it is derived from, is actually "*enthousiasmos,*"[1] which comes from en (in) and theos (god) the God within—divinely inspired. And he always distinguished between inspiration versus motivation: Motivation is getting ahold of an idea and taking that idea where you think it needs to go. Inspiration is almost the opposite. Inspiration is when an idea gets ahold of *you* and takes you to the point you needed to be all along. He said that when you feel enthusiastic about something, it is not merely an excited or happy emotion; it is literally the Divine, God, the universe getting a hold of you and guiding you along to honor what it is you are called to do. In other words, enthusiasm is not excitement; it is

God reminding you of what you came here for, what your dharma is—it is honoring the Knowing that we each feel when we allow ourselves to be guided, even in the face of doubt, that we are honoring our inner voice, the one that never lets us down or leads us astray.

BUMPS

One of the best early examples of our parents encouraging us to follow our intuition comes from when Saje was about five years old. She developed a rash on her face. When it became clear that these bumps weren't going away on their own, our parents took her to a doctor. The doctor diagnosed the bumps as "juvenile" or flat warts and told our parents they shouldn't be concerned—they are pretty common in kids, and they would heal on their own in the next few weeks. When Saje heard the doctor say that they were warts, she announced she would only call them her "bumps" and made our parents promise they would not tell anyone—especially the other kids in the family—what they really were. Something about the word *wart* didn't sit right with her, and she felt like it would invite some teasing. Our parents agreed, and hence they became her bumps.

After several months, it was clear that these bumps were not getting any better and in fact were becoming worse, so our parents took Saje back to the doctor to see what could be done to treat them. The doctor explained that the treatments for flat warts were harsh. He could either burn them or freeze-dry them, both of which would be painful and could leave some scarring. He could prescribe an oral medication, which might or might not work, and had several side effects, including itching and peeling skin and the need to stay out of the sun. None of these options sounded at all appealing to her now-six-year-old ears, so she asked our parents if they could continue to wait and see if the bumps would heal on their own. Our parents almost always honored the choices we made, even from this young age, and since they knew that these flat warts were not causing her any harm, they did not force her to treat them.

The truth was, the bumps did not bother Saje. At that age, she did not look in the mirror and judge her appearance, and the only thing she remembers is how the skin on her face never felt smooth. But after almost two years of waiting, the bumps had in fact only gotten worse. At this point, they had spread towards her eyes and become more inflamed. Saje was a kid who spent a lot of time outdoors, and since the warts didn't contain pigment, they became more pronounced when her skin would tan.

Our parents once again took Saje to a doctor, this time a specialist, a dermatologist out in Maui. This dermatologist confirmed the original diagnosis of flat warts but told us it was time to treat them. He said that her immune system was not fighting the virus that caused them. He outlined the same two options that the other doctor had given us: either burning them off or taking an oral medication with tons of side effects. Saje listened to this doctor and understood what he was saying but was adamant that she did not want to try either of these options if she did not have to.

Our parents chatted in private with the doctor for a few minutes. When they returned, they told her that they had come up with a third option. Saje could talk to her bumps and heal herself using the power of her mind! The doctor just stood there, neither agreeing nor disagreeing with this third option. It felt like a pretty easy decision for her to make, and she told the grown-ups she was going with option number three: healing herself of her bumps.

That night, she got into bed and spent about five minutes talking to the bumps. She fell asleep and essentially forgot about it in the morning. She repeated this practice for the next two nights—talking to her bumps for five minutes before falling asleep. On the fourth night, she got into bed and started to talk to her bumps, but then she stopped, because when she reached up to feel her face, they were completely gone! The skin was smooth, without a trace of the "bumpiness" that she had grown accustomed to for the past three years. She jumped out of bed (actually off her air mattress, because the youngest kid always got the air mattress) and ran into our parents' bedroom, bouncing onto their bed and exclaiming, "They're gone! They're gone!" Our parents weren't quite sure what she was so excited about and asked what was gone. *Her bumps!* Our dad took a closer look and was shocked. "Oh my God, they are gone!" Our mom examined her face as well, and neither of them could believe that in just a matter of a few days, these warts, which had been on her face for years, were completely gone without a trace.

Dad immediately asked her what she had said to the bumps that made them go away. Saje was a little embarrassed and told him that it was a secret. He started to tickle her and continued to ask what she'd said to them, but she insisted it was a secret. They went back and forth for quite some time. It became a game, and Dad became desperate to know what she had said. He even tried to bribe her, offering ice cream or twenty dollars to tell him what she'd said. She kept refusing, because she enjoyed the game and the attention but also because she was a little embarrassed to share something that felt very personal. Dad even sat her down, telling her this was material for his work, but she still wouldn't tell him! He had our mom and siblings try to catch her off guard by asking what she said, but that stubborn little girl never once wavered. Eventually Dad pretty much gave up.

Years later, when Saje was in high school, she realized there was no need to keep this bumps thing a secret anymore. She decided she would reveal to Dad what she had said to her bumps. She told him she'd told her bumps that she loved them but that they couldn't live on her face anymore. She thanked them for coming to her and being with her, and she asked them to now leave. She emphasized how much she loved them—they'd been a part of her—but she also kept picturing herself with clear, smooth skin.

When she told Dad this, she was surprised by how emotional he became. He said he was amazed that on her own, as a young child, she had decided to use love and compassion to heal herself, and he was convinced that was the reason talking to her bumps had worked. He called the dermatologist, who we were still in touch with, to tell him that she had finally revealed the big secret, and the dermatologist began to cry. Saje remembers him saying that he had imagined that she had threatened her bumps and told them she'd be waging war on them if they did not leave. Saje never really realized until that moment how profound her healing had been. Because she chose to approach a "problem" with love, the universal intelligence within her body responded positively.

Another reason Saje believes that talking to her bumps worked was because as a little girl, she totally and completely believed it would. She had no doubt, and that absence of doubt is another way to describe her Knowing that she could and would heal herself of her bumps. At that age, having our parents tell her that this was her third option was enough of a reason for her to believe in its effectiveness. If someone told her to do this now (parents or not), and she had never had this experience with her bumps as a child, she would likely harbor some serious doubts. She would probably still be willing to give it a try and might even try to convince herself that it could work, but as a child, she had no doubt. She knew that she could heal herself.

As adults, we try to remember this example of the power of the mind, which can be applied to far more than just physical ailments and illnesses. It happened because our parents encouraged Saje to connect with her own truth, her own Knowing.

DEFINING MARRIAGE

Indeed, growing up Dyer was idyllic . . . until it wasn't. When Saje was eleven and Serena sixteen, our world was flipped upside down when our parents announced, completely unexpectedly, that they were separating and divorcing. It was the first time we realized that life can change in an instant.

In June of 2001, our mom put us—our brother Sands, who was thirteen years old at the time, and our friend Lauren (who was around so much that she might as well have been a Dyer)—on a plane from Florida to Maui to be with our dad. Mom said she would join us in a couple of weeks after she took some time to go on a silent retreat and reflect on certain upsetting things that were going on in her and Dad's marriage.

When we got to Maui, we realized our dad was distressed by everything that was happening, and we made it a point to help out as much as possible. Serena had just gotten her driver's license, and with that newfound freedom, we kids were able to spend many afternoons exploring Maui on our own for the first time. Sands begged her to drive him to surf spots on Maui, and she would agree, so we all piled into the minivan to check out a new beach while Sands surfed. Saje always wanted to volunteer at the Maui Humane Society, so Serena, Lauren, and Saje would drive over there, drop Saje off for a few hours, and then return later to get her, as Saje would have spent all day, every day, with those dogs if she could.

This was the first time Serena felt what it was like to be in charge, without a parent driving her everywhere and paying for everything, so in some ways, she was forced to grow up and fill in the role of "mom" while our mom was away. This meant food shopping, cleaning the condo, managing the grocery money, and making dinner. Making dinner became the highlight for her, and it was this summer that Serena really began to cook, a passion of hers that exists to this day. As Serena was navigating her new role, she often clashed with Saje, who did not enjoy her sister trying to be a parent. Despite our many battles that summer, we ultimately grew closer, as Serena eventually realized she didn't need to be Saje's mom; she just needed to be there for her.

Mom never came to Hawaii that summer. The four of us stuck together, and taking care of our dad became a priority, as it was increasingly clear that our normally ebullient and enthusiastic father was on the verge of depression. Dad couldn't get out of bed, and overnight it seemed like our world had been turned upside down. He would talk on the phone for hours with Maya and Reid, his assistant and publisher, and we would overhear him lamenting our mom leaving him. What he was not doing was acknowledging that he had played the biggest part in our mom deciding to end the marriage. When we would get on the phone with our mom, she would defend her decision not to come to Maui. Our parents did not shield us from what was going on or why. There was never an attempt to hide the truth from us, and because of that, we never blamed ourselves for their divorce. We knew why our mom wanted it, and we understood. As hard as it was to accept, we did.

By the middle of the summer, it seemed that everything was going to get better, because our parents were talking on the phone several times a day and ending their conversations with "I love you." One afternoon, on the way back from a boat trip to the island of Molokini with our dad, our mom called his cell phone. He pulled over to a beach on the side of the road so he could talk to her and let us kids out of the car.

While we were on the beach, we picked up large rocks and tried to skip them on the ocean's surface. Sands threw a rock frisbee-style toward the shore, and as he did, Saje, not realizing, walked in front of it. The rock slammed into her head with a sickening smack. Blood started spurting everywhere. Serena ran across the beach as she ripped off her T-shirt and used it to apply pressure to Saje's head. Saje had collapsed, and blood was gushing. Serena picked Saje up and carried her to Dad. When he saw what had happened, he shouted "Saje!" and dropped his phone on the sand and sprinted to her.

After handing Saje to him, Serena picked up the phone and heard our mom screaming "What happened to my baby? What happened to my baby?" Serena told her she couldn't talk because Saje was bleeding everywhere and hung up on her. Serena was upset and wanted to focus on Saje and use the phone to call an ambulance. She was also angry that her little sister was hurt and that our mom wasn't there to make it better. If she had been, she would have known exactly what to do, but because she wasn't, Serena felt the burden, even though she was just a kid herself.

We met up with an ambulance, and the EMT carelessly examined Saje, telling us that it was a minor abrasion and to apply a butterfly bandage and wash it when we got home. When we got back to the condo, Serena started to wash Saje's head. When her finger slipped deep into the wound, she realized the cut was much deeper and bigger than we had originally thought. When we arrived at urgent care, Saje looked at Serena and asked her to promise she would not let the doctor shave her head for stitches. As an eleven-year-old girl about to start a new school, Saje was terrified of losing her hair.

Serena promised she would not let them, just as the doctor came in and announced the wound was quite deep and Saje needed *two* layers of stitches and they would have to shave a three or four-inch patch on her head. Serena grew hysterical. "You can't! I promised her! She's starting a new school soon, and I promised." Saje was inconsolable too. The doctor and our dad asked Serena to leave the room and told her she was making things worse. And she probably was, but for her sixteen-year-old self, there was nothing more important in that moment than keeping her promise to Saje.

When we finally got home from the doctor's office, Serena noticed that Sands was barely talking and seemed to be fighting tears. He was acting as though he felt ashamed. He choked back sobs as he told Saje he was very sorry for throwing that rock. In that moment, Serena felt like everything she knew and loved, everything that was precious and sacred, was crumbling along with her parents' marriage.

Looking back, Saje's head injury was a turning point in our parents' relationship. It marked a shift from coming at each other with attorneys, threats, blame, and fear to making a pact to approach the divorce with love. And this love served to dissolve the divorce altogether. Eventually, all attorneys were fired, and the word *divorce* was no longer spoken. Our parents realized their relationship did not have to adhere to any societal standards. As soon as our parents decided to call off the divorce and become friends again, their relationship grew, and they became exponentially closer as each year passed. They stayed married until the day our dad shed his physical form. Their marriage might not have looked like a typical one; they both saw other people and lived in separate homes. However, they still came together as a family several times a year in each other's houses, on vacations, and even on stage to share the love they had for each other. They spoke on the phone daily and very much parented their children together, often referring to each other as best friends. Having parents who could love each other in the face of their differences served both of us as a beautiful example of the power of putting your ego aside and choosing love.

A Way of Knowing

If you choose love,
life will respond with love.

Having our mom and dad separate rocked our world, but even as children and teenagers, we chose to focus on moving forward and not staying stuck in a desire that was outside our control. As children living through our parents' uncertainty in their marriage and trajectory toward divorce, we had a choice in our own response and attitude toward this situation. Witnessing our parents choose love during this difficult time showed us that we can always choose love and that life will respond from there. We learned from them that we could use love in every situation, even ones that appear the opposite of love on the surface—like divorce—by processing life as it was and not as we assumed it should be. After all, life is not happening to you; it's responding to you.

It could have been easy to play the victim and create a "poor us" situation. But we were not raised to put any value on this sort of mentality. We were not victims of our parents' divorce. Instead, we were witnesses to the complications that can arise in marriage and then to the miracle of choosing love. Upon reflection, we never perceived this time in our life as a big challenge, and because (thanks in no small part to the behavior our parents modeled) we chose for it to be easy, it was.

We witnessed a new and different kind of love evolve between our parents and ultimately as a family, and this became not a moment of sorrow and pain but much more than that: a moment of realizing that we could in fact choose how to respond to what was happening, even if we could not control it. As Viktor Frankl wrote in *Man's Search for Meaning*, "Everything can be taken from a man but one thing: the last of the human freedoms—to choose one's attitude in any given set of circumstances, to choose one's own way."[2]

Our mom and dad chose their own attitude, and as unconventional as it was, it was one of love. We, as kids, witnessed firsthand the transformative experience that choosing love, kindness, forgiveness, and acceptance over everything else can have and how making that shift from anger and resentment to love and forgiveness can change a difficult time into one of profound growth and healing. The entire experience changed not just for our parents or our family but also our understanding of how freeing it is to decide for yourself how to respond to any situation you encounter.

The energy that you bring to every moment of your life will determine the feeling you walk away with. If you are coming from love, life will respond with love. Every situation can be perceived as an opportunity to grow or an obstacle to keep you from growing. The choice is ultimately yours. In every conflict that arises in your life, ask yourself, "Am I coming from a place of love?" Even in situations where we do not feel a person deserves our love, we are challenged to get to a point in our lives where we come from love *not* because someone else deserves or doesn't deserve it but because love is all we are in ourselves, and therefore it is all we have to give away. Our dad frequently summarized the Taoist principle by saying, "The sage is kind to the kind, and kind to the unkind, because kindness is his nature."

Our dad used to hold up an orange on stage and ask his audience if he squeezed it, what would come out? Of course, everyone answered, "Orange juice." And then he would say, "If someone squeezed you, what would come out? If you are in a situation in which there is conflict, what will come out of you? Is it love or fear, anger or hatred? Whatever you carry around within you is what emerges when you are in difficult situations, or when you are 'squeezed,' so become a person that only has love to give—carry that inside, and only that. When Jesus was being crucified and the Roman soldiers robbed and mocked him, he responded with, 'Father, forgive them; for they know not what they do.'"[3] That is the highest form of divine living that one can attain—to offer forgiveness to someone while they are in the act of harming you. Certainly neither of us have reached this goal of a lifetime, but we know it is one we should all seek: becoming Christlike and carrying only love within us and being able to realize, as Ram Dass, our dad's mentor and spiritual friend, often taught, "I am loving awareness."

So what do you do when you are feeling "squeezed" and something other than love is coming up for you? Or when you are experiencing something that seems loveless on the surface? We'd like to offer an idea that is inspired by the childhood wisdom of Saje's "bumps" story. When you find yourself experiencing something that is causing you to feel hurt/upset/disappointed or anything that just doesn't feel good, try sitting down and writing a letter to your problem. You might be saying to yourself that you have no idea what you would say to your problem that could in any way come out positive, but that is okay. Just start writing anyway. Often, the inspiration and clarity lie in the actual writing process. We can't tell you how many countless times we have sat down to write with the feeling of writer's block looming, only to end up writing some of our most inspirational pieces and leaving the writing process feeling as if we found the clarity we were seeking. Getting this clarity through writing can help to shift the energy of the problem itself and start you on the path of healing instead of staying stuck in the problem.

CHAPTER 3

The Mind Forgets but the Soul Remembers

"What catches our attention might be more
than a coincidence—it might all be a potential
incident of inspiration . . . I think of the word
inspiration as meaning 'being in Spirit.'"

DR. WAYNE W. DYER,
LIVING AN INSPIRED LIFE

TUITION INTUITION

Before our dad passed on, Saje was in a master's degree program at NYU, studying psychology and counseling. She had two full years to go before completing the program. She was fortunate enough to have a father who could afford to pay for her to go to graduate school, and this he did. Our dad had a very precise way of handling the money she needed to pay her tuition and also to live on for each semester, and basically it went like this: each January and September, Dad would write her a check that included the money she needed for that semester. It was her job to pay the tuition and budget the rest so that it lasted the entire semester. Our dad had used the same system for all seven of our siblings, whom he had already put through college. So in January of 2015, after Saje spent the holidays out in Maui with him, Dad followed his routine and gave her a check that was enough to last until September. She expressed her gratitude for his continual and selfless gift of education, and a few days later, she packed up her things and headed back to New York City to begin the spring semester.

Only a handful of days had passed when Saje received a call from Dad. He did not sound like himself. He was in a somber mood, and he spoke in an uncharacteristically serious tone. It was unusual for our dad to embody anything other than love and joy, so this struck her, and she responded by being serious in return. On this call, our dad told Saje that he had mailed her a check for the remainder of her master's program—four semesters in total—and he instructed her to deposit the check and to make absolutely certain that she budgeted and made the money last during the two years for which it was intended.

Saje was baffled by this. First, we had a system that worked perfectly well, and he had been implementing it for more than twenty years, since he put our oldest sister, Tracy, through college. Second, it was a *huge* amount of money, more money than Saje had ever had at one time in her entire life, and she did not feel comfortable accepting such a large sum. When she expressed her feelings to Dad and told him that she would feel much more comfortable continuing to do things the way they always had, he spoke seriously and said, "Saje, I instruct you to deposit that check. Do not question me on this."

When she pressed him and asked him to at least give her an explanation for the sudden change, he said, "If anything were to happen to me, I want to ensure that you can finish school. I made a promise that I would put you through graduate school, and I intend to keep that promise."

It was upsetting to hear our dad talk like this. Saje hated to think of even the possibility that something could happen to him, and especially something soon. She told our dad she didn't like that he was talking like this, that nothing was going to happen to him, and she asked him one last time if they could keep doing things the way they had been doing them. She told him she would rip up the check when she received it in the mail. But once again, he insisted. And even though it made her uncomfortable, she agreed.

She called our mom after she got off the phone with Dad and told her what he had said and what he was doing. Saje explained to Mom that it was upsetting to hear our dad talking like this and that she wished he wasn't making her deposit this check. Saje was hoping Mom would say that he was being dramatic and that everything was fine, but she didn't. She insisted that Saje listen to our dad. Mom is an extremely intuitive woman, and we would bet her intuition was telling her that it was important Saje listen to what our dad was telling her.

When Saje received that check in the mail, she went to the bank and opened a separate account so she would be sure to budget it accordingly and not mistakenly believe she had more money than she really did. Nine months after that phone call took place, on August 30, 2015, our dad left his physical body. Saje believes the higher part of him had a Knowing that the day was coming.

WITHDRAW

Saje wasn't thinking about school during the summer that preceded our dad's passing, however. She had published a book about her bumps story and traveled to Australia and New Zealand with our sister Skye and her husband, Mo, and our dad on his speaking tour. When dad invited Saje on stage, he always introduced her as "Withdraw" and told a funny (and highly embarrassing) story. In Saje's words:

> I'm sure my dad is getting a real kick out of the fact that I am about to explain my own conception story, but here goes: In 1989, my parents were traveling throughout Australia on one of my dad's speaking tours. They brought along their two youngest children at the time—Sands, who was over a year old, and Serena, who was three years old. On the night of my conception, they were staying at the Hilton hotel in Brisbane, and in their room, they had two queen-size beds. Mom, who was still nursing Sands, slept in one bed with him, while my dad shared a bed with Serena.
>
> As the story goes, in the middle of the night, my Mom got up, acting as if she was in a sort of trance. My dad described her behavior as extremely odd and very unlike her. She started rearranging some of the furniture in the hotel room and eventually picked sleeping little Serena up out of my dad's bed and moved her into the bed with Sands. My dad was flabbergasted and asked her what in the

world she was doing and why at three o'clock in the morning. She didn't answer but proceeded to climb into his bed and initiate "things."

Now, my parents had had four children in the past eight years, not to mention their three older children, so they were definitely not trying to have any more kids. Mom had actually been told by her doctor that she very likely would not conceive again because of complications with her ovary (she only has one). My dad told me (and every audience I ever spoke to with him) that even though they had been told they probably would not conceive again, he still wanted to take an extra precaution, and so he withdrew at the critical moment (gag).

Whenever my dad told this delightful little story, he always emphasized this was simply not behavior typical for my mother. Not only had she never before initiated "things" in the middle of the night—thanks to all my siblings, she had been sleep deprived for pretty much the entire decade of the 1980s, and sleep was something she never gave up for anything. My dad described her as being "in a trance" and very unlike herself. Mom remembers the night in the same way and always says that she does not know what came over her. Anyway, I am the product of that encounter in Brisbane. I defied the odds and was conceived—as the result of a "withdraw," which is how I landed this cute little nickname.

Our dad's whole point in sharing this before he brought Saje on stage (aside from being a bizarre icebreaker) was to emphasize that she got here under circumstances in which the odds were stacked against her. She had big dharma to fill.

NEXT PHASE AND EVICTION

Saje will always treasure that last trip to Australia—the funny, loving, profound moments with Dad, Skye, and Mo and the immersion in her father's teachings as she attended hour upon hour of talks. He often lectured about the beauty of death, describing it as a world of infinite love. Presented with a choice of ending grief for a loved one sooner or later, he always advised that people "choose sooner" and dwell in a place of love. During that trip, Saje's perception of death shifted, and she began to understand how we are neither our bodies nor our minds.

Looking back, there were lots of indications that our dad knew on some level that his time on earth was coming to an end. After he gave his last talk in New Zealand on August 27, 2015, Skye, Mo, and Saje all walked Dad out past the rush of people who had attended his lecture and over to a back entrance, where a car was waiting to take him to the airport. We kids were booked on a different flight the next day, since Dad would be returning to Maui to write and we were all heading back to the East Coast. We each took a turn giving our dad a hug and telling him we loved him before he got into the car and we waved him off to the airport. Saje had no idea on any conscious level that it would be the last time she ever hugged our dad and told him she loved him to his face.

After saying their goodbyes, Saje, Skye, and Mo went out to a restaurant to get dinner and celebrate the last night of an amazing trip. That was when Skye and Saje received the following text message: "You guys were both stellar tonight. I am always so proud when you're on stage. I am in the lounge. Looking forward to some rest from this long eviction. Phase 1 is now complete. Love you both so much. Dad."

Saje responded: "Thanks, Dad! I had such an amazing time this whole trip. It was so fun getting to travel with you some more and I'm always so awed by how hard and dedicatedly you work. Have a safe flight. I love you."

He answered: "I love you, 'Withdraw.' I'm so happy you insisted on getting here. You really shine onstage. This is a trip none of us will ever forget. I love you infinitely. Dad."

Saje replied: "I'm so happy too, and that is NOT my new nickname. I love you so much."

Dad's final text to Saje said: "Withdraw Dyer is WD. Same initials as your Daddy. On the plane now. Going seepy soon."

When Skye and Saje read that first text message from Dad, they said to each other that they felt like there was something off about what he had written and wondered if there was indeed a deeper meaning to "Looking forward to some rest from this long eviction" and to "Phase 1 is now complete."

Just to give a little background, our family home on Maui is a condominium, and the building in which it is located was undergoing some major renovations that year. The entire complex had to be shut down for four months to replace water pipes and air conditioning units. No residents could live in their homes for the duration because it was a major construction site, and hard hats and protective clothing were essential.

Knowing this, it's easy to believe that when our dad said "long eviction," he was referring to his eviction from our home on Maui. (Even though when he returned to Maui from Australia, he still could not return to his condo for a few more months, so he went to a nearby hotel.) It's also easy to see our dad saying "Phase 1 is now complete" as meaning Australia and New Zealand, the first phase of the many trips he had lined up. But when Dad left his physical body less than seventy-two hours after he wrote these words, they took on a different meaning to all of us.

Reading the texts after Dad's death, we understood this message in an entirely different way. When he referred to his "long eviction," his human side might have been referring to his long eviction from Maui or our condo, but when we read it now, we believe his higher self knew his time was coming, and he was perhaps referring to his "long eviction" from Heaven and from God—what he would call our "true home." Our physical bodies can make us feel like we are separate from each other and God and contribute to thinking from a "What's in it for me?" perspective, but Dad taught us that when we leave these bodies, we realize we are all one. We end our long eviction from this Knowing and from feeling the love of the infinite universe.

It's easy to see his choice of words as a coincidence and nothing more, but our dad liked to remind us that the word *coincidence* is derived from the mathematical term *coincide*, which refers to two angles that fit together perfectly; it's a misuse to define it as two things that come together accidentally. In a world with no accidents, everything is on purpose. Our dad's choice of words in his last text message to Saje and Skye is not a coincidence. These meaningful words helped us realize his higher self knew his time was coming. There was never anything accidental about them, and now we began to put the pieces together that his seemingly random and sudden passing was in fact divinely orchestrated. These realizations lead us to the conviction that he knew his time was coming.

MOM'S LAST CALL

Skye and Saje weren't the only ones. Our mom and dad talked pretty much every day, and their last phone conversation lasted for more than an hour. It was Friday evening in Florida, and Dad had just gotten back to Maui after his Australian speaking tour. He told Mom how much he missed her when he was traveling, and they spoke as they often did about their love that was so strong even though they had separated. This time, they congratulated each other that they had done it—remained best friends and in love.

Then, suddenly, he said, "I have made amends with everyone but one person."

This was odd to hear, and our mom asked out of curiosity, "Who do you need to make amends with, Wayne?"

He told her it was a former literary agent he had worked with decades ago. They had not spoken in many, many years after this man's father had died. Mom reassured him there were probably no amends necessary, given what she knew about that situation, and that this man still loved him. Dad's bringing this subject up felt strange to her.

After that, Dad spoke to Mom's partner, Tony, as well, and they both said they loved each other. He told Tony how much he respected him and appreciated his care. It was a very nice conversation, one that left all of us full of love and goodness.

Dad called the next evening, but she missed his call. He died that night.

Our mom will always believe Dad had a Knowing about his death. It might not be perfectly defined, but she knows he was sincerely saying his goodbyes.

THE DESIRING AND
ALLOWING CONTINUUM

Sometime after our dad passed away, Dee shared some things that led her to trust that our dad knew his time was coming. You should know that our dad *loved* his plants. He talked to them daily, and if one of us was going to be at the condo on Maui without him, he gave explicit instructions on how his plant-babies should be watered and tended with love. Dee said that when she was helping Dad pack before he headed to the airport, he looked at her intently, then took a minute to look around the condo, really soaking it in. At the time, she thought this was because he wouldn't be returning there for a few months while it was getting worked on, but looking back, she thinks he knew that he would never be returning there again, because as they were getting ready to leave, he turned to her and said, "You know what, Dee? I want you to get rid of my plants." She was surprised—she knew how much he loved those plants. She asked him if he was sure, and he said, "I won't be needing them anymore. Just give them to someone who will take care of them."

She went on to tell us that right before Dad got into the car to head to the airport on the Australia trip, he had tears in his eyes as he looked around the whole property, which had been a home and such a special place to him and our entire family for years. It was as if he was taking it all in for the last time. And it turned out he was—he never returned there again.

Dee also told us how after they wrote their book *Memories of Heaven*—extraordinary stories of children having memories of Heaven and being with God—together, Dad told her that the process had given him even more conviction that we are indeed spiritual beings having a temporary human experience (instead of the other way around). He said writing this book allowed him to feel a new excitement for what he called the "next phase." Dee found it odd that he would say that he was excited for death, because once, after watching a documentary on prisons, she had asked if he had to choose, would he rather spend life in prison or receive the death penalty? Our dad responded that he would choose life in prison because all life is valuable, and there is always more to learn and opportunities for true spiritual growth.

When we asked Dee if she was sure that Dad had used the words "the next phase," she assured us that was exactly what he'd said. Dee knew for certain because she had spent a lot of time contemplating the seeming paradox of our dad valuing life but being ready for that next phase.

If there had been any shred of doubt that our dad's words in that text message had been coincidence, this evaporated it. What Dee shared solidified our faith that when Dad was referring to "phase 1" being complete, he meant his life in this physical realm was coming to an end.

We all contemplated the seeming paradox of our dad stating that he valued life, yet he was ready for the next phase. This idea would come to mind at different times throughout the first year following our dad's death. During that time, Saje decided to read *Change Your Thoughts—Change Your Life*, Dad's book about living the profound teachings of the Tao Te Ching, written by the ancient Chinese philosopher Lao-tzu. She wanted to savor it, because every single page is full of wisdom, and she felt like she could read each chapter for a month and see something new every time. She decided to study each verse for four days straight before moving onto the next of the eighty-one verses. She got this idea from our dad. When he wrote this book, he spent four days studying, meditating on, and living each verse before writing the chapter for that verse. So on the first day she started the book, Saje read the preface and the first chapter, which are all about how the Tao is filled with seeming paradoxes to get you to change the way you look at your life. In the first verse, Dad explained that in the West, we "tend to view opposites as incompatible concepts that contradict each other" but that in order to live the great wisdom of the Tao, we must transcend this ingrained way of thinking and open up to view paradoxes as "mysterious ends of a continuum." Our dad could convey this concept far better than we can:

Desiring is the physical expression of creating con-
ditions that allow us to be receptive; that is, it's
in-the-world preparation for receiving. According to
Lao-tzu, wanting to know or see the mystery of the
Tao will reveal evidence of it in a variety of manifesta-
tions, but not the mystery itself. But this isn't a dead
end! From this ground of desiring, the flowering of
the mysterious Tao grows. It's as if wanting transforms
into effortless allowing. Desiring, one sees the mani-
festations; desireless, one can see the mystery itself.[1]

This paragraph helped Saje understand what Lao-tzu (and Dad!) meant with all his seeming paradoxes. Instead of seeing the Tao as a collection of opposites—such as "you can't allow if you are desiring or wanting"—you can see them as necessary components of each other, like yin and yang. To get to the place of allowing, you must first have the desire; they go hand-in-hand. For instance, you can have a desire to go to sleep because you are tired, and this will bring you to get into your bed, but sleep will not come from this desire; you must then allow it to occur. If you have a desire in your life, that's the first step. Then beginning to allow that desire to take place in your life is the second. As our dad often said, "Let go and let God."

After reading this section of our dad's book about paradoxes and our ingrained ways of thinking, Saje thought back to the paradox that Dee had shared. This idea that Dad valued life to such a high degree, yet he was ready for the next phase, all seemed to make a lot more sense. Valuing life and being ready for what comes after life are not mutually exclusive ideas. Since death is a part of life, it's a matter of allowing our lives to unfold as they are meant to while letting go of the desire that everything stay as it has always been. Saje came to see that it was our dad's emphasis that life is valuable and meaningful combined with his desire to live this life and make it valuable that allowed him to be ready for the next phase.

NUMBERS AND SYNCHRONICITY

Our dad loved synchronicities and numbers and often found meaning in times of day, dates, or even his Social Security number. It was a way he gauged alignment with the universe. It was a game, but it was also a lesson in how bringing something into our awareness makes it show up more often.

During Saje's last summer in Maui with Dad, one of his favorite little number games was to notice when the clock read 11:11, because he appreciated the synchronicity of four repeating ones. He was pleased with himself whenever he "coincidentally" caught the time at 11:11, and after he set the intention to see this, he noticed it practically every day. If at any point we spotted an 11:11, we were instructed to immediately tell him or text him at that exact moment so that he wouldn't miss seeing how we were all in alignment. It was a fun little game, but it was also a lesson in how what you choose to focus on grows.

Another numbers game our dad enjoyed had to do with the number 18. He loved when 18 showed up, because for him, it represented all the power of the universe, standing for 1 ∞ (infinity), or one infinite source. He taught us that that's all there is. No matter our spiritual teachers or religion, there's only one infinite source from which we all originate, return to, and exist in right now. When Skye and her husband, Mo, were looking at houses, he was excited when one of their final choices had the address 909, because it added up to 18. He joked that this was a sign for them to go with that one, and they did.

During his last summer on Maui, Dad went for a run every day. He wore a digital watch and set the timer for 30 minutes. When he was at the eighteenth minute, he would pause and attempt to get the stopwatch to land at 18:18:18. Then he would continue his run. Each day, when the timer neared the eighteenth minute, he would stop running and attempt to hit the pause button at the exact moment the digits reached 18:18:18 (minutes, seconds, hundredths of a second). He tried to do this for six months and even got within one one-hundredth a couple of times, but he was not able to stop at the exact 18:18:18 mark. Finally, one day, he did it. He was so excited! He even stopped his run to take a picture of his watch and sent it to the entire family with an email announcing:

> "I've been trying for six months, every day, to get my stopwatch to stop on triple eighteens, today, December 1, 2014, I finally made it happen. The timing is exquisite here, I have to stop the watch to the hundredth of a second. For months I've been at 16, 17, 19, 21, etc., but today I was able to hit the jackpot and stop it on the hundredth of a second that was in my universal infinite consciousness of a mind. Big big day . . . (I've got to get a life) Love, I AM WAYNE (the infinite timer)."

Although this is a funny insight into our dad's dorkier side, our real point in sharing this is to convey that he was always looking for signs and ways to pay attention or challenge perspective. When Dad died, our family believed that there must be some significance to him leaving this earthly plane on August 30, 2015. If there truly was divine order, our dad would not have died on just any old day, so we often wondered, what was it about this day that made it special? What was the hidden message here?

Then Saje made a discovery.

I knew in my heart that on some level the date of our dad's death would have meaning. At first, I couldn't figure it out. There was no significance in the number 30 or the month he died. I tried adding all the number up to see if they totaled 18 or some other number he always loved, but nothing appeared. Until I finally saw it.

It was after I decided I would read my dad's last major book, *I Can See Clearly Now*, which was the only one he wrote that was in the form of a memoir. I chose to read this book first because I wanted to be immersed in the stories of his life. I also wanted to read this book because I was with my dad during the entire summer he wrote it.

I was spending the summer of 2013 on Maui with Dad, Sands, and Sommer. On June 26, our Dad sat us all down and announced that he had decided he was finished with writing. He told us he felt he'd had enough years of the pressure of filling blank pages with words and that he had written everything he had inside of him. I was a little surprised to hear him say this, but I also felt he deserved to be done. He was in his seventies, and if he wanted to spend the rest of his life working a little less, then I was perfectly fine with that.

However, on June 27, my dad started writing—despite his big declaration the previous day. In the morning when I saw him sitting at his "sacred writing space" (a.k.a. our family dinner table), I started laughing. Of course he couldn't stop writing, because sometimes we are called to do something, and this calling is far more powerful than the decisions of our ego. The book that he began that day was *I Can See Clearly Now*. I had never seen him so compelled to write before in my life. He told us he really did not know why he was writing this memoir now, but one thing he knew was that he was being called and compelled to write this book to the point that he could not stop the ideas from pouring out of him.

When she read *I Can See Clearly Now*, Saje found the answer we were all looking for.

MEANING OF AUGUST 30

When our dad was a child growing up in Detroit in the early 1940s, his father abandoned our grandmother (his wife) and her three sons—David, Jim, and our dad—and never looked back. Melvin Lyle Dyer was an alcoholic and not a great husband to begin with, but he did at least help to pay the bills for their family. When he left, our grandmother was on her own, trying to figure out how to care for three small boys and provide for them financially. For a woman in the 1940s during World War II, and as the effects of the Great Depression lingered, this proved an impossible feat, which is why our dad ended up living in various foster homes and orphanages for a few years. Eventually, our grandmother was able to regain some stability, and she succeeded in reuniting her family.

By the time Dad was a teenager, he'd become curious about his biological father but also enraged that he had left his family with nothing and without ever looking back. Dad spent many angry years searching for answers, having dreams that ended in rage-filled violence. He was desperate to confront his father and to ask if he had any love in his heart for his sons. His mother refused to tell him anything beyond what an awful person his father was and how they were all better off without him. It almost became an obsession over the years, always creeping into his dreams. He even volunteered to be a pallbearer at his fraternal grandmother's funeral, believing that there was no way his father would miss his own mother's funeral. He was once again disappointed, though, because his father never showed up.

Finding his father became a fixation for our dad, and for years, even when he thought he had put it all behind him, the anger kept him stuck. Eventually, after decades of searching, in 1964 he learned from a cousin that his father had died of liver failure in New Orleans, and his body was buried in Biloxi, Mississippi—but there was no information about where. Although this news might have put some sort of closure on our dad's search and need to know his father, it didn't do anything to heal his pain and answer the question of why the man had abandoned the family in the first place.

Ten years later, he experienced a series of remarkable "coincidences." Dad was teaching at St. John's University in NYC and was offered an opportunity to earn some extra money by evaluating a teaching program in Columbus, Mississippi, to make sure it was in compliance with the Civil Rights Act. He was excited that his business trip would give him a chance to look for his father's grave. After his work was completed in Columbus, he rented a car (odometer reading 000.000.8) for the two-hundred-mile drive and, weirdly, found a business card in this brand-new car. It was for the Candlelight Inn in Biloxi. When he arrived in town, he found three cemeteries listed in the phone book. He called each one and, on his final try, discovered where his father was buried. Our dad asked for directions and was stunned to learn it was in a cemetery for indigents on the grounds of the Candlelight Inn, the very same place listed on the random business card he'd found in his rental car!

He found the grave. Still carrying anger and hatred for his father, he had every intention of quite literally pissing on it. He stood there for hours, sobbing and yelling and letting out some of that anger that had built up in him over the past thirty years. He demanded answers until he had nothing left to ask. And then, as he described it, a calmness came over him, and our dad began to feel some relief. Even more amazing, he began to sense his father's presence around him. And this presence felt like pure love. He turned to walk back toward his car when he felt an urge to return to the grave and declare forgiveness to his father.

In no way was that his intention for this day, but he described it as an indescribable force that beckoned him back as he said out loud, "I want you to know that I can no longer think hateful thoughts about you. When I think of you now, it will be with compassion and love. From this moment on, I send you love."

In that moment, he was a changed man. He experienced an undeniable *Knowing* that he had participated in a miracle. He abandoned the rage he had held in his heart toward his father for most of his life. His situation didn't change—his father was dead, and they would never have a relationship—but that moment of looking at things differently made all the difference. His life and remarkable career took off from there as he went from being a victim to being empowered.

The day our father's relationship with *his* father changed and shifted his entire life?

August 30, 1974!

Here is how he put it: ". . . if asked what is the most significant experience of my life, I respond with the events of August 30, 1974—being at my father's grave site in Biloxi, Mississippi, forgiving and loving him, and cleansing my soul of the toxicity that living with internal rage had brought."[2]

Before that date, our dad's life was pretty unfulfilling. He was overweight, in an unhappy relationship, doing work that wasn't always rewarding, and suffering from nightmares about his father that were so violent he'd often awaken in a cold sweat. He knew that there was more to *his* life, but he felt trapped by his own circumstances.

After the events of August 30, 1974, these things that had left him feeling unfulfilled shifted. He changed his diet and began exercising and getting his health back. His writing took on a whole new meaning for him, and he wrote his first bestselling book, *Your Erroneous Zones*, in just two weeks. He ended his marriage and made way for new love (which is eventually how we got here). Overall, his life became meaningful, and by connecting to his Knowing, he began to truly live his dharma of teaching and helping others.

Dad's transformation can be credited to the power of true and profound forgiveness. It wasn't until he was able to forgive his father and send only love instead of the hatred that had previously dominated his mind (changing the way he looked at things) that his life changed. When you forgive, when you reach a place of true mercy, you lose something to gain something even greater, doing it with no expectation of anything in return. Yet often what you receive from a place of forgiveness is unimaginable from the standpoint of nonforgiveness.

August 30 marked one of the most important days in Dad's life and represents the day his relationship with his father changed. When we realized that our dad also departed from his physical body on this exact same date, forty-one years later, we were amazed by the meaning that we were able to draw from this, and it caused a shift in *our* perspectives. We believe that by dying on this same day, August 30, Dad was saying to all of us that this was not the day that our relationship with our father ended; it was the day that it shifted to take on a whole new meaning, just as it had for him with his father. It is up to us to nurture this new relationship and make it one of pure love instead of looking at this date as a tragic loss marking an unfillable void in our lives.

TURNING POINT

August 30 marked one of the most important dates in Dad's life not because his external circumstances had changed but because his inner self did. When we realized that Dad's soul must have chosen this date to depart from his physical body, we sought out the lesson it taught. It was not the day our father-daughter relationship ended; it was the day when it shifted and took on a whole new meaning, just as it had with his father.

A date that could have marked the worst day in our lives has instead become a day to celebrate our new relationship with our father as we embody his teachings and make them our own. More than ever we are constantly seeking an understanding of the messages the universe sends.

Coming to see our dad's passing as a change in our relationship with him but not the end of our relationship has made an extraordinary difference for us. At first, his death was final, and it meant that our life with him had ended. Thinking in this manner was devastating, and it made growth impossible. We dwelt on the fact that we could not talk to him, could not receive comfort or a laugh or advice, and would never actually *see* him again. These types of thoughts created turmoil. However, learning to view his death as merely a transition and a change has turned this experience into one we can grow and learn from. When we think about our father, it is no longer "I can never see him or talk to him again," but instead, perhaps when we catch the time as 11:11 or spot the number 18, we ask ourselves, "What is Dad trying to tell us now?"

A Way of Knowing

Become a host to miracles instead of a hostage to circumstances.

After thirty years of rage, our dad shifted from anger to love in an instant. It's our reminder to seek out a path that leaves hatred and anger behind, no matter what type of storm might be swirling around us. Our dad's shift from hatred to love, although it built for more than thirty years, took place in an instant. Our dad used to talk about "satori" moments, or moments of instant awakening, and how these instant awakenings are available to all of us if we choose to *allow* them to happen. It is the difference between staying attached to anger and honoring that quiet nudging of your soul, inviting you to choose peace instead. There are constant, daily miracles present for all of us, and we may often find them in coincidences and synchronicities. But the true test is whether we can stay committed to receiving this Knowing. This is where the challenge and the miracle abide.

The lesson for us here is that believing in the otherworldly or synchronistic is a choice. It can be challenging to choose to see the light when we are constantly challenged by logic and by what we perceive with our five senses, but making the conscious decision to believe makes you a seer, one who sees, and the signs and miracles flow from there. Don't waste your energy trying to change the immutable, because there are no accidents in a perfect universe.

You have to show up and do the work. That's something our dad would say: signs or coincidences are divine guidance, but what we do with them is up to us. So often, especially when we seek out spiritual meaning in experiences during crises or difficult times, we want the solution to be laid out for us. We want our problem to be fixed, but we don't want to have to show up and do the work ourselves. We place the power outside of ourselves rather than recognizing that ultimately, to receive any of this guidance, this inspiration, this connection to your highest self and to all that is missing in your life, you have to show up and be truly open to receiving it. It all comes from going within. If you're seeking a higher connection to God, to the part of you that is God, to finding what's missing or fixing what's broken in your life, the only way to do that is to become *like* what it is that you're seeking.

That's what our dad did when he forgave his father. He went to his father's grave to find peace from all the anger and resentment that had been building in him over the years, but his focus was still on expressing the anger and crying over the abandonment. Our dad was ready to leave and be done with his exercise in blame and anger, pointing the finger at the father he never knew. But when he felt that quiet urging of his soul, that little voice encouraging him to go back to the grave and send only love and forgiveness from that moment on, our dad did not ignore that inner voice and think, "This guy doesn't deserve my forgiveness. I'm not giving him love when he never loved me while he was alive and I was his son."

He didn't justify his anger and resentment (as justified as it might have been), because ultimately, he wanted to be free of the anger building inside of him toward his father. Ultimately he wanted peace. When that inner voice, the quiet urging of his soul, called him back to the grave so that he could finally find peace in all of it, he honored it. When he honored that inner calling, he found himself only able to give his father love, and that choice he made, to abandon the anger and replace it with love, was what made all the difference in the world. And that choice took place in a single moment, a moment of instant awakening.

When we choose the broader perspective of trusting that each and every one of us is on our own path, a path that gently encourages us to return to love for no one else's benefit but our own, that is where we open ourselves up to the idea of changing the way we look at a situation, and as a result, the situation itself changes. And isn't that what we are seeking all along with whatever difficulty comes our way? Aren't we all seeking a way to find that inner peace, no matter what storm is churning up the delicate aspects of our lives?

Making the commitment to becoming a host to miracles instead of a hostage to circumstances is as small as making a daily commitment to not react, not judge, not condemn whatever difficulties come our way, or to notice things the universe sends us, like 11:11. Of course, we all want the transformation that our dad experienced when he was standing on his father's grave, but for some of us, the shifts happen through slow and sometimes painful growth. A satori moment, a miracle, a change in our perspective from what is to what could be—those are the constant, daily miracles that present themselves for all of us. But the true test is whether we can stay committed to receiving these—that is where the challenge lies.

So what can you actually do to stay committed to receiving? We encourage you to notice the moments when alignment occurs for you, whether it's as simple as seeing the clock at 11:11 (or any other time you set your intention to) or something bigger, like receiving a phone call from the person you've been wanting to talk to but haven't been sure how to reach out to.

Whenever you notice a moment of alignment, big or small, say a quick prayer of gratitude such as, "Dear Universe, thank you for these moments of alignment that confirm I am on the path to all of my desires." Bringing your present-moment awareness onto gratitude can be the catalyst that shifts you from the desiring end of the continuum to the allowing and ultimately receiving end of the continuum. Because when you're aligned with gratitude in the present moment, you set your desires into motion, allowing them to transpire.

CHAPTER 4

From No Where to Now Here

"Go through life continuously grateful and
appreciative—give thanks for all of nature and
the multitude of miracles you see appearing
before your eyes each and every day."

Dr. Wayne W. Dyer,
Excuses Begone!

JUST MY LUCK

In discovering the meaning behind August 30, we were
set onto a path of viewing Dad's death as a meaningful
and on-purpose event as opposed to a tragic and prevent-
able accident. With that shift, signs and miracles flowed
that continued to focus our perspective. We were raised
to believe that there are no accidents, and in the days following our dad's passing, this upbringing served us as we
both experienced Knowings that his death was in divine
order, and he could still guide us.

For our dad, it wasn't only about numbers; our parents were open to all sorts of signs of alignment with the
universe. One of the most wonderful gifts we received

from our dad was his reversal of the old saying "Just my luck." Instead of blaming the universe for the bad in life, he celebrated its good.

If he found a quarter on the ground, he'd accept the gift from the universe, saying, "Just my luck!" According to Serena:

> I started adopting that. So if I found a good parking spot, I'd say, "Oh yes, just my luck!" One of my friends said to me, "You realize that you say that wrong every time?" I remember looking at her replying, "Do you realize that you do?" She explained, "People say 'Just my luck' when they mean 'Oh shoot, something bad happened.'" To which I replied, "I know. But I was raised to say 'Just my luck' when something good happened to reaffirm to the universe that I am lucky and that good things happen to me because I expect them."

"DO YOU KNOW HOW BEAUTIFUL YOU ARE?"

A few nights before our dad's public memorial service in Orlando, Saje had a bizarre dream. In it, she was dreaming but doing exactly what she was doing in real life—in bed in New York with her little dog Pixie, getting ready to start her day. She heard the door to her apartment open, so she sat up to see who it was. There was our dad, walking toward her with a mischievous grin on his face. He smirked and said, "Hey . . ." in a funny sort of way. He was wearing swimming shorts and no shirt—which was pretty much what he always wore when he wasn't on stage. He looked about ten years younger than the last time she had seen him. Saje jumped out of bed and ran over to him but stopped before she reached him. She asked, "Dad, are you really here?"

"Yes. I'm really here."

"Dad, I know I am asleep right now, but this is *not* a dream. This is as real as anything that happens to me when I am awake."

When our dad responded by assuring her that it was indeed not a dream and that he was there, Saje felt many things at once—excited, emotional, confused—but then her skeptical mind kicked in. She stopped and said, "Okay, Dad, if you are really here, then I should be able to touch you."

He laughed and looked at her lovingly as he replied, "So touch me!" in an exasperated sort of way. Saje grabbed each of his arms with her hands, and she *felt* him! She felt his warm skin and his hairy arms—exactly the way he felt in real life. At that moment, she gave in, dropped her skepticism, and hugged him. They both laughed as she asked him where he was and what he'd been doing. He told her he loved her and that he was always with her (and all of us) and that she needed to focus on her work, because down the road, she would be doing what he did.

When Saje's alarm went off, she awoke, sat up, and said to herself, "That was *not* a dream." It was more real than she can convey. She knew she had been with our dad and has never been surer of anything.

A few nights later, Saje was working on a paper for school and was inspired to send a message to a medium and psychic counselor named Karen Noe, whom she did not know very well at the time but had met recently at our dad's celebration of life in Orlando. She explained her dream and asked Karen if she had any insights. It's important to note that for her entire life, Saje has been both a skeptic and a believer in things like mediums and psychics. We grew up with parents who were *extremely* open and who were constantly doing and talking about "weird" things, which naturally caused us to be open to them. However, for Saje to believe anyone truly has an ability to connect with someone on the other side, they better knock her socks off and say something that *only* she would know.

In the note to Karen, Saje described her dream and asked her if she had any thoughts. Karen wrote back almost immediately and told Saje that her dream was most definitely a visitation and asked if she could call her. Saje missed our dad desperately and was still coming to terms with him not being here physically, so an opportunity to connect with him evoked an immediate yes!

When Karen called, she conveyed a message from our dad, affirming that Saje had a real mission to accomplish in this physical world. They spoke for several minutes, and Karen suggested an in-person appointment at her office in New Jersey. She explained that she was booked for appointments more than two years out but that she would find a time to squeeze Saje in because she felt compelled to share with her. They set a date for about a month later, which turned out to be when our mom, Skye, Serena, and baby Sailor would decide to visit her in New York. Saje laughed, knowing that it was no "coincidence" that their trip happened to fall on the day she had her appointment with Karen.

A month later, Mom, Skye, Serena, and Saje drove from her apartment in New York to Karen's office in New Jersey. In the car, we took turns saying what we wanted our dad to address if he were to really come through Karen, and we each made a point that it had to be more specific than someone would be able to find on social media. Serena wanted our dad to say something about her daughter Sailor, something about her husband Matt's legal situation, and whatever else he wanted her to know. Skye said she wanted our dad to say something to her about a white bird that showed up in a dream as well as on her patio a couple of days earlier—was it a sign?

When we arrived at Karen's office, she seemed different from how we remembered her. She announced that our dad was already with us, that he couldn't wait to get started. We were all excited, but our mom and Skye had to use the bathroom, and we remember Karen telling them where the bathroom was and then clearly, distinctly, in the exact same tone and inflection as our dad, saying, "C'mon, let's *go*, we have to get moving, let's go, let's hurry up," as if she were actually rushing our mom and sister to finish up in the bathroom. It was *so* like our dad, just like the countless times we heard him say those *exact* words when we were kids and going to be late for school. It sounded so much like him, and the delivery was so similar, that it felt as if our dad was in the room, communicating through Karen.

When we all sat down to get started, Karen explained how our dad's energy was different from that of other people she had channeled. She said he felt light, he felt very loving. He was loud and strong when he came in, and she said he was beyond excited that we were there and he would get to communicate with us. Right off the bat, she explained that he had been coming to each of us and was constantly with us but that it was difficult for him to get clear messages through while we were sad, when we weren't matching his joyful, loving energy. He said that it would be much easier for him to reach us if we would meditate, but in the meantime, he would continue to visit us in our dreams, since our energy was more open there. Karen (or our dad, if you will) then looked right at Skye and said, "By the way, since you were wondering, yes, I sent that bird to your home so you would correlate the bird on your patio with the one in your dream—it was my way of saying hello."

After Karen's bird comment to Skye, which was exactly what she had asked our dad to address on the way over, Serena was convinced that Karen really was hearing messages from our dad. So you can imagine her shock when Karen turned to Serena and said, "Congratulations!"

Congratulations for what?

Karen looked a little perplexed and said, "Oh, well . . . congratulations because you are pregnant."

Serena's jaw hit the floor. She told Karen that the whole pregnancy thing was probably a mistake—she currently had a baby and was doing everything in her power not to get pregnant. Sailor was six months old, and it felt as if she had given birth just yesterday. Our mom, Skye, and Saje looked at her accusingly, as if Serena had withheld the news of her pregnancy from them, so she immediately said, "You guys, this is crazy. I am *not* pregnant! I will take a pregnancy test when we get back to Saje's apartment to prove it!"

Karen was adamant, though, smiling and laughing, saying, "Oh dear, you really are pregnant!" Then she went on to say, "Your dad is talking about the Fourth of July—something about fireworks." In her desire to change the subject, Serena explained that he was probably talking about how on the Fourth of July, we were always together on Maui and how Sands and our dad loved to set off fireworks.

Throughout the remainder of the meeting, it became increasingly clear that Karen had the gift of communicating with our father. She told Serena that our dad was constantly playing with and talking to Sailor and that he loved how funny she was, which was the same thing he told her while he was alive. She said that Serena's husband's legal situation would end in our favor, and she said more times than anything else how much our dad wanted our mom to know how much he loved her.

At one point, in the middle of a sentence, Karen stopped, looked right at our mom, and said, "Do you know how beautiful you are?" We all started crying, feeling like we were in a scene from the movie *Ghost*, because our dad used to do that all the time—stop in midsentence and ask one of us if we knew how beautiful we were. Here Karen was, speaking for our dad, and she did the exact same thing. Karen said, "Oh my, so you know, Marcie, that was Wayne! I think you are beautiful too, but that was Wayne saying that!" We laughed and cried some more. The experience was so real, so pure; no one could have known our dad did that with his wife and sons and daughters.

As you might imagine, when we left that office, we stopped at a drugstore to get a pregnancy test for Serena.

> I took it, and sure enough, it was positive. My due date? The Fourth of July. I guess that's what those firework references were about. Little Windsor Wayne made her debut on July 1, 2016—Matt's and my two-year anniversary. I couldn't help but think Dad had a hand in it all.

THE MOUTHS OF BABES

Once we opened ourselves up to the signs, we found them everywhere, like the time at a family barbecue on Maui when Dee's son, Marcus, who had known our dad for all two and a half years of his life, looked up at the sky and out of the blue said, "Wayne gone. Wayne gone . . . Wayne home." It was so simple and honest, the way children are, that it felt as if Marcus was able to see and hear our dad trying to let us know that he was home, happy to be wherever he was, and it was as simple as that. Dee wasn't fazed—she told us that Marcus often made comments like "I miss Wayne" or "Wayne home, Wayne gone." Shortly after our dad passed, she bought Marcus a large box of crayons, and when Marcus opened the box and saw all the colors, he exclaimed, "Wow, Mommy! Wayne's colors." When Dee pressed him about it, he explained that Wayne looked like all these colors now, and he left it at that.

Marcus wasn't the only child who connected with our dad. Serena discovered that Sailor could communicate very clearly with him as well. She regularly went over to the bookshelf in their home and picked one book to carry around, as if it meant something more to her than the others. After noticing her do this a few times and ignoring it at first, it occurred to Serena that the book she was always choosing was one of our dad's books about meditation: *Getting in the Gap*. When Serena picked it up from Sailor's little hand and opened it, she remembered that this was in fact the book that our dad had dedicated to her many years ago. Inside, he had written, "Serena, this book is dedicated to you. Stay in the gap. Whenever you feel lost or hurt, it will reconnect you to God. I love you—Dad."

Another time, as Sailor awoke from a nap, she began making baby noises, and it sounded like she was talking. Serena looked over at her daughter and noticed a pure-white feather stuck to her shoulder. Sailor kept babbling in a way Serena had never heard her speak before. She asked, "Sailor, is that a feather? Are you talking to your grandpa?" In her sweet little voice, she clearly replied, "Yeah," and then continued smiling and cooing.

MOLTING SEASON

There were more feathers in our future. When someone told Saje that our loved ones often let us know they are with us by presenting us with feathers, she started to see and find feathers everywhere—on every single sidewalk, stuck to trees, or floating in front of her. At one point, she even took to Google to look up whether it was pigeon molting season in New York City. Was it possible that she had been coming across these feathers all along and had not been paying attention to them? It was. She still feels that each one is a little "hello" from our dad.

Saje is a natural-born detective, so you could say that she wasn't all that surprised when her boyfriend Anthony proposed. Of course she said yes! And of course she was excited, but she also experienced something no amount of detective work could have uncovered. As soon as she told our family the news and the congratulatory texts and calls started to pour in, a surprising sadness came over her. She knew that if her engagement had happened six months earlier, our dad would have been the first person she would have reached out to, and now she wanted to talk to him more than anything else in the world. Saje wanted to hear his voice and share his joy at learning his "baby" was engaged to be married, yet she couldn't.

But she did not want this moment to be sad. She didn't want this feeling for herself, but even more, she didn't want it for Anthony. This was a special time, and it was a day they would remember for the rest of their lives. The last thing she wanted was for it to be anything but joyous. So she told herself she wouldn't go into sadness. Instead, she got quiet and asked our dad to give her a sign to let her know he was there. She asked that he connect her to her Knowing and show that he had not gone anywhere, only his body had. Once she asked for the sign, she looked behind her, and sticking up in the grass was a giant, pure-white feather. She couldn't help but smile. She and Anthony spent the rest of that day smiling and celebrating, and our dad was right there celebrating as well.

THE HOUR I FIRST BELIEVED

It's experiences like these that can change the entire direction of your life. *A Course in Miracles* describes a miracle as *a shift in one's perception.* Our dad loved to tell the story he called "Saul to Paul" from The Acts of the Apostles in the New Testament. It began when Saul of Tarsus was traveling on the road from Jerusalem to Damascus on a mission to arrest the early disciples of Jesus and bring them back to Jerusalem to face punishment and imprisonment.

> *Now as he was going along and approaching Damascus, suddenly a light from heaven flashed around him. He fell to the ground and heard a voice saying to him, "Saul, Saul, why do you persecute me?"*
>
> *He asked, "Who are you, Lord?"*
>
> *The reply came, "I am Jesus, whom you are persecuting. But get up and enter the city, and you will be told what you are to do." The men who were traveling with him stood speechless because they heard the voice but saw no one. Saul got up from the ground, and though his eyes were open, he could see nothing; so they led him by the hand and brought him into Damascus. For three days he was without sight, and neither ate nor drank.[1]*

According to the story, God sent a disciple named Ananias to Saul and told him to lay his hands on him and restore his sight. Ananias was reluctant, because he knew how vicious Saul was toward the Christians, but ultimately, he relented and did as God asked, saying, "Brother Saul, the Lord Jesus, who appeared to you on your way here, has sent me so that you may regain your sight and be filled with the Holy Spirit." Ananias's act of grace led to Saul's instantaneous conversion. His entire view of Christianity shifted in an instant (a miracle!), and as a result, his entire life changed as well. Saul transformed into Paul, later known as the Apostle Paul, and went from being an eradicator of Christians to being one of the first Christian missionaries and great theologians.

Another example of miraculous transformation Dad loved was that of Captain John Newton. It's said that Newton was transporting slaves from Africa when his ship was swept into a terrible storm as it approached Ireland and began to sink. Terrified he would die along with all the people he held captive, Newton got down on his knees and prayed. The storm passed, and so did his ability to treat his fellow humans as chattel. He turned his ship around and sailed back to Barbados. He released the slaves and is said to have dedicated himself to becoming one of the era's most ardent supporters of the abolition of slavery.

Later, in 1772, Newton wrote the lyrics to "Amazing Grace."

> . . . I once was lost, but now am found
> T'was blind but now I see.
>
> T'was Grace that taught my heart to fear
> And Grace, my fears relieved
> How precious did that grace appear
> The hour I first believed.

Paul and Newton, like our dad when he forgave *his* dad, experienced a satori moment, a moment Buddhists would call "sudden enlightenment" and what we call the Knowing, a reconnecting to the inner compass that we are all born with. But many of us spend our entire lives ignoring it or avoiding heeding that gentle nudging of our inner, highest self. The key thing to realize here is that no matter how you label them, these miracles are opportunities to shift our perception from seeing the conditions of our lives, the things we don't like or perceive as curses or faults of ourselves or others, to seeing them as gifts and blessings. The opportunity for this kind of shift is constantly available to each of us if we make that leap—if we pay attention. We can't stress it enough: the ability to receive one of these miracles is available to each and every one of us on a daily basis.

We believe these men were transformed by changing their perception of what was occurring in their lives, and in doing so, they were instantly free. Of course, it is easy to look at miraculous shifts that took place almost instantly and come to the conclusion that although those miracles might have occurred for those men, they aren't available to regular people like us in our day-to-day lives. However, we were raised to *know* that these miracles are constantly present in our lives, but it takes awareness and commitment to receiving one in order for the miracle to present itself in the first place.

Serena recalls that one of dad's favorite verses from the Tao Te Ching included the line "Yielding is the way of the Tao."

There are situations and crises and tragedies and fears that we all are going to experience in our lives. In each of those tragedies or situations I found myself in I had to contemplate the question that I heard our dad ask so many times: "Do you want to be a hostage to your ego or a host for God? The choice is yours." So much of what we experience in life is the result of the story we tell ourselves about ourselves. Are we a persecutor or a liberator? It's also the story we tell ourselves about the world in general. It is only when we release the ego and yield to the divine that the Knowing arises.

For most of us, the shift is not instantaneous. We must constantly make an effort to find the *opportunity* in these challenges, or tests, such as learning to respond to hate with love or to judgment with compassionate nonjudgment. We need to remember that from an early age, we're taught to perceive with our five senses and operate from our mind. But there is an alternative, which is to completely know that beyond the five senses is a whole realm of guidance and inspiration and signs that are waiting for us. It may come in the form of feathers, unexpected babies, or flashes of insight. When we turn away from the mind and into the Knowing, we can have a shift like Saul to Paul, and these miracles are waiting for us.

A Way of Knowing

Our dad's Knowing came from embracing what is rather than what should be. Instead of "I'll believe it when I see it," he always emphasized that "I'll see it when I believe it." Our experiences after he died led us to this same realization and to a turning point for both of us.

Don't believe everything your senses tell you. If we only relied on what we can see, hear, or touch, we would be cut off from the entire mystical experience of connecting to not only our loved ones on the other side but an entire belief system that teaches us how to become like what it is we are seeking. When Albert Einstein said, "It is better to believe than to disbelieve; in doing so you bring everything to the realm of possibility," he was speaking to the notion that when we believe in a world of possibilities, we become the creators of what it is we are desiring.

Seek out ways of finding the meaning, looking for the connection to something bigger than yourself at play, because each of us has the ability to choose how we respond to what is happening in our lives. Do we respond by becoming perpetually limited by the circumstances we find ourselves in? Or do we look to the deeper meaning of it all, trusting that the universe is guiding every moment and there are no accidents? After our dad died, we both knew this was a fork in the road for us—would we become reduced or transformed by this experience? Would we stay in the morning, never advancing to the evening without our dad there, or would we use this to propel ourselves more into our own discovery of connecting to that inner Knowing, trusting that it was not an accident at all?

Have you ever contemplated that everything we know about this universe we know because of our five senses? Our whole world is shaped by what we see, what we smell, what we hear, what we touch, and what we taste. We have no other ways of perceiving our surroundings, and therefore all information arrives through one of these five senses. Of course, there are people who can't see or who can't hear and so on, but the people with these types of disabilities tend to rely more heavily on one of the other senses. And there are also people who have a more developed "sixth sense," but for the most part, we as humans perceive our world with the five senses.

These five senses tell us everything, and we rely completely on them for all our information about our surroundings. However, we already know that these senses deceive us. For instance, your body is telling you right now that you are sitting in a fixed position, reading this. However, we know that that is not entirely true. You are in fact sitting on a planet that is hurtling through space and rotating on several axes at once. These senses not only deceive us, but they are limited. Our eyes can only see so far out in the distance; our ears can only detect sounds within a certain range; there must be a certain number of molecules of a scent present for us to detect it with our noses. Eyewitness testimony is some of the least reliable testimony out there, because our minds often put their own little spin on what our senses detect.

Not only do our senses deceive us, and not only are they limited, but they can omit information about our surroundings. For instance, if we think about it, we know that right now there are AM and FM radio waves coursing through the atmosphere, including in the room that we are currently sitting in. If we were to turn a radio on, it would easily pick up on hundreds of radio stations being broadcast at this very second. But because we are not radios and do not have an antenna with the capability to detect radio signals, we have no idea that these radio waves are present. We don't know what they "feel" like, nor do we have any way of detecting them—and therefore, we usually forget or fail to acknowledge that they are there.

This is how we like to think of our loved ones who have passed on. Most of us do not have that "sixth sense" that allows us to hear or see someone who has passed away (or at least we aren't tapped into it), and because of this, it's really easy to get down in the dumps and feel like they are truly gone. But we already know that our five senses deceive us and that they fail to report everything in our environment and that they are limited. So isn't it fair to say that there are probably millions of "things" in our universe that exist, but because we don't have a perception mechanism to detect these "things," then we assume that they aren't there? Our dad is truly the first person we lost in our lives whose loss hurt to the point of changing us. Prior to losing our dad, many of these ideas and beliefs about the "afterlife" and so on were things that we were familiar with (especially growing up with the parents that we had), but because they did not really apply to us, we never gave them much thought. Losing our dad forced us to take a closer look at what our beliefs were about how this universe works.

The reason we received and continue to receive signs is because we are open to them. When you open yourself up to the universe, the universe opens itself up to you. This is not just a matter of feathers or (as we'll share later) faces reflected in the ocean. Believing in the otherworldly—what's beyond the veil, the mystical, magical, or even the holy—is a choice, but if you make it, you become a seer, and the signs and miracles flow from there.

A friend of ours lost her mother suddenly, and for years she would argue that she never received any signs, either because they weren't real or because her mother wasn't giving them. We would gently urge her to consider that perhaps her mother was giving her signs, but she was so attached to receiving them in the way *she* wanted that she was missing the signs that were already there.

After years of believing that she had not received a single sign, she agreed to talk to a friend of ours who is a gifted medium, Sarah-Renee. After the initial reading with Sarah-Renee, our friend said that she felt the reading was okay, but she wasn't blown away. This was really surprising, because many friends who had worked with Sarah-Renee were given "without a doubt" messages from their deceased loved ones, messages that were so specific no one could have known about them from a Google or social media search.

It wasn't until a year later, when our friend became so open to receiving signs from her mother that she found herself actually vocalizing her desire for a sign, that, sure enough, she got one almost immediately. Even better, she decided to go back and listen to her reading with Sarah-Renee, which she had recorded. Upon listening to it again, she realized that she had been so closed off to actually receiving messages, even though she convinced herself she was desiring them, that she didn't pick up on all the specific "without a doubt" signs that she had been given during her reading with Sarah-Renee.

When she finally got to the point in her life that she was actually ready to receive signs and messages from her mom, when she was truly open to whatever form they came in, with no attachments about what they *ought* to be, sure enough, she began to receive constant signs, messages, and guidance from her mom. It took her years, but her persistence paid off, because once she truly abandoned the fear and became completely open to receiving, the signs poured in. In fact, they had already been pouring in, but it was only from the change she made in her own perspective that she was able to really begin receiving them.

One of the greatest tools we were taught to embrace by our parents was the gift of our imagination. Everything that exists now was once only imagined. Everything you would like to create or align with or become is available to you, but you must first imagine it. Before bed, rather than scrolling through Facebook or watching TV, take the last five minutes before you drift off to actually imagine yourself experiencing what it is you desire. Don't just picture it; feel it. Feel what it will be like when you are in the place you dream of being, and feel the sense of peace you will have when what you are seeking is actually present in your life. Rather than allowing your subconscious mind to marinate in everything that went wrong with your day over the next eight hours of sleep, bring into your mind and your body the feeling of what it will be like when you have what it is you are desiring. In doing so, you become a vibrational match to whatever it is you want, and the universe cannot help but bring you what you are in alignment with.

Our five senses are limited, but our imagination is not. Rather than living from the space of needing to see to then believe, turn it around and believe, imagine, feel what it is you are seeking, and then you will experience it. Our thoughts are energy, and the energy we send out into the universe is the energy we receive back. As our father said many times, we do not get what we want, we get what we are. Are you in harmony with what you are seeking? If the answer is no, we encourage you to imagine yourself as such, to really feel it, and then operate from the knowing that what you are seeking is already on its way. Just remember, as our dad often said: "Miracles come in moments. Be ready and willing."

CHAPTER 5

Stars in Daylight

" . . . deciding to make things a bit more bearable by
making [people] laugh or inviting them to have fun
instead of being sad, is—on a spiritual level—the
same as writing books about breaking free of the trap
of negative thinking and enjoying life to the fullest."

DR. WAYNE W. DYER,
I CAN SEE CLEARLY NOW

ROUND-TRIP TICKET

Dad often spoke about how we come to this earth with
a round-trip ticket, and we don't necessarily know when
the date of our return will be, but we do know that it
will come. Almost everyone on this planet celebrates
the first leg of that trip. A new baby brings hope and
new beginnings and is considered pure and uncorrupted,
and we continue to celebrate our birthdays for the rest
of our lives, giving recognition to the anniversary of our
entry into the physical world. Yet many of us spend a
great deal of our existence fearing departure, the day the
return ticket comes due, either for ourselves or for our

loved ones. Death is surrounded by the unknown, and the unknown often incites fear.

We were both fortunate to get to hear our dad speak and give lectures for much of our early lives into adulthood, and we've come to truly believe that the universe has a guiding force through which we connect to our Knowing. This guiding force that causes us to be born at the right time—an event few people ever question—is the same guiding force that calls us back. For us, this means that we should not question with our egos when we or our loved ones are called to leave. We come here on time, and we leave on time. Death can be one of the hardest things for us to deal with, and yet it has happened to every person who ever lived, and it will happen to every single person who is alive today. Our dad often said that the tragedy is not that death happens; the tragedy is that we interpret it through the lens of "this shouldn't happen."

Growing up, we bore witness to both of our parents losing their parents. Our dad lost his mother when he was in his seventies, and our mom lost both of her parents about a decade apart, in her fifties and sixties. While both of them grieved during these difficult times, they also had the immediate reaction of happiness that their parents, whom they loved so dearly, were on to the next great adventure. Saje can recall our dad saying that he envied those who had entered this mysterious next phase. While of course still feeling excited about his life here in the physical realm, he had a genuine knowing that what comes next is a submersion into love beyond our wildest dreams.

After our dad left his physical body, it did not take us long to realize that he most certainly knew on some level that his time was coming. We're not saying he was aware on a conscious level, because we do not believe that he was, but there was a part of him that Knew. We believe that there is probably a part of all of us that senses when our time is coming, and Dad was not the type to run in fear from this reality. Instead, he embraced it.

REALLY, REALLY, REALLY

Serena's last phone conversation with Dad was on the day before he died. They caught up after his Australia trip, speaking about how happy he was to be back on Maui and how he was looking forward to going to Europe with her and some of the family the following month. Then, as their conversation was winding down, it took an odd turn. Dad said he wanted Serena to make sure she always looked after one of our sisters who has struggled over the years. Serena said, "Of course I will. I always will." She remembers him insisting, "You know, it's just really important that you always make sure that you reach out to her and make sure she feels your love."

Then, as they were saying their goodbyes, Dad said something that surprised Serena even more: "The ocean looks so beautiful . . . I just want to go for a swim."

Serena asked him, "What about what that guy said?"

Swimming was something our dad had done daily for years until a few months earlier, when he was in Canada with Skye and saw a healer for his neck pain. The healer had told our dad it was no longer a good idea for him to swim in the ocean and that the next time he did, he would die. When Dad told us about it, we took it to mean that if he went in the ocean, something would happen in the ocean—a heart attack while swimming or a collision with a boat. He had been feeling nervous during his ocean swims for a while and couldn't figure out why, so when the man told him he needed to stop, it resonated with what he had been feeling, and he stopped. After that, he swam his laps in a local pool instead.

Dad told Serena, "You know, I'm just not attached to that. If it's my time, it's my time. I'm totally at peace with that." He no longer seemed concerned by what the healer had said. If it was his time to die, he was prepared to go. The ocean looked beautiful, and he wanted to be in it.

As they were getting off the phone, Serena remembers thinking that you can't always buy into what other people say anyway, and she said, "Alright . . . bye, Dad. I love you." Just like she always said it.

He replied, "Serena . . . Serena, I love you. I *really* love you and I want you to know that I've always really, really, *really* loved you."

Serena wondered why he said it so many times. Later, it occurred to her that she hadn't been able to travel for those three weeks in Australia with him because she had four-month-old baby Sailor, and it felt like he made a point of connecting with her one last time.

Now, when she recalls that call, she appreciates that on a deep, subconscious, Knowing level, he was aware he was going to leave his physical body soon and made a point of saying goodbye to her for the last time and telling her he really, really, really loved her, as if he were driving that point home once and for all.

PERCHANCE TO DREAM

For the three weeks before our dad left his physical body, Saje had been traveling with him, our sister Skye, and Skye's husband, Mo, throughout Australia and New Zealand. They were on a Hay House tour in which our dad gave lectures in four different cities throughout the two countries. Our sister Skye would sing a few songs at each of my dad's lectures, and Saje would get up on stage with him for twenty or thirty minutes and share her "bumps" story. Since Skye and Saje were technically part of the show, Hay House, being the exceptional company that it is, not only paid their way on this trip but also paid for them to travel in the most luxurious way—up in first class with our dad on every single flight. Our dad's travel agent knew that if seat 2B was available on the airplane, then that was the seat that our dad wanted, because he loved to joke and say, "Am I in seat 2B, or not to be?" He was in seat 2B on almost every flight they took on that trip.

Now, Skye and Saje were not used to this first-class treatment and would get very excited on all of the flights because they were truly treated like queens. The seats on the airplane laid back into beds, and they were given pajamas for the flight, champagne whenever they wanted it, a menu to select delicious meals, TVs with endless shows and movies of their own choice—the list went on and on. Our dad LOVED to joke with us about this first-class treatment that we were getting, and he would look over at Saje on the flights and tease her by saying, "Oh, are you enjoying yourself over there with your TV and your champagne and your lay-flat bed? It must be nice!" Or he would tease us and say, "You realize that the ONLY reason you are sitting on this airplane right now is because of me, right?" Or he would say, "Now, you little bratanellas better not get used to this first-class treatment, because it's a ONE-TIME thing." Our dad loved to tease us, but of course it always came from love, and we all developed pretty good senses of humor thanks to him.

Mo, Skye's husband, was not a part of the Hay House show, and therefore he paid his own way to get to and around Australia and New Zealand. So he (unfortunately for him) did not join us in first class but instead sat back in coach on each of our flights. Naturally, those of us in first class boarded the airplane first, and it became one of our dad's favorite things to tease Mo as he walked past us on the plane to get to his seat in the back. Dad would say, "Mo, do they even have seats back there, or do you all just have to pile up and hold on for dear life?" Or he would say, "Don't worry about us, Mo. We'll just be up here in first class, and I'm sure we'll find you when the flight's over." Dad was always making us laugh, and this trip was no exception. Eventually, it became one of the running jokes of the trip to tease Skye and Saje about their first-class treatment and Mo about his lack thereof.

Now fast-forward to the morning of our trip to Maui, just a few days after our dad had died. At four in the morning, Saje and Serena, along with Matt and Sailor, headed to the airport (the rest of the family was on a different flight the next day). Serena and Matt, who were on a separate reservation from Saje, checked in first and got their tickets.

We were flying on Virgin America, an airline that Saje had only flown one time prior and with whom she had no frequent-flyer status whatsoever. So after they checked in, Saje went up to the counter and handed the ticket clerk her ID to be checked in. After the clerk typed on her computer for a few minutes and tagged Saje's bag and put it on the conveyer belt, she handed Saje back her ID and her boarding pass and said, "Have a great flight. Enjoy first class." Saje looked at her and said, "Excuse me?" She thought she was hearing things, but the clerk repeated, "Enjoy first class." Saje slowly took her ticket and ID from the clerk and managed to say thank you through her confusion. Then she took a closer look at her boarding pass and saw that she was in seat 2B.

In Saje's own words,

> In that moment, I knew my dad had had a hand in this. There was no other explanation for why my reservation ended up being a first-class ticket. I looked back at my credit card to make sure I hadn't been charged for the seat, and I hadn't. I asked Serena if she just decided to be nice and generous and pay for my upgrade, and she assured me that she DEFINITELY did not do this. I could feel my dad smiling and joking with me almost as if he was saying, "Okay, fine, I'll get you first class just this one last time." And on a deeper level, I felt like my dad was letting me know that even though he's not here physically anymore, he would still always be taking care of me, just as he did when he still had his body. Tears welled in my eyes as this Knowing sank in.

Saje and Serena's plane landed in Maui at night, and as they descended, Saje couldn't stop noticing how bright the stars were in Hawaii. She had been living in New York City for the past two years and couldn't remember ever having seen a star in the Manhattan sky—they're obscured by the artificial light and tall buildings. The stars weren't something she consciously missed, but for whatever reason, that first night back on Maui, they captivated her, and she could not stop staring at them in awe.

Eventually, she went to bed at the condo and fell into an exhausted slumber, catching up on some much-needed sleep. The next morning, after breakfast, she played with Sailor and then walked down to the beach to get some sun in the very place where our dad used to swim, even on his last day in his physical body. This Knowing gave her a burning desire to immerse herself in the water. She decided to swim out into the ocean and follow the route that our dad always took. If you are familiar with Kaanapali beach in Maui, Dad started in front of the Westin Hotel and swam north to Black Rock or south, depending on the tide. When Saje was about fifty yards from shore, she started to think about sharks, a thought she always had when she was far out at sea. This thought, however, was immediately replaced by the realization that she now had the best guardian angel she could ask for. She trusted our dad would not let harm come her way, and if it did, then it was her time.

She continued swimming until she was out of breath and couldn't go any farther, turned back, and returned to the shore, where she lay down on her towel to dry in the bright Hawaiian sun. While she lay there, she opened her eyes, squinted at the sky, and realized she couldn't see the stars. She thought, *Well obviously you can't see the stars right now, because it is daylight and the stars are only visible at night.*

Then another thought popped into her head: *Just because I can't see the stars right now doesn't mean that they aren't there. In fact, if I think about it, I know that the stars are still there, because they are always there. I can't see them because of the physical limitations of my body to only see stars in the nighttime.*

Then she heard a voice that sounded like our dad. *Exactly, Saje. You can't see the stars right now because your eyes don't have the capability to see stars in the daytime, but you know that they are there. That is exactly how I am now; you can't see me, but you must know I am here. In fact, I'm everywhere, and I will never leave you.*

As she lay on that beach, tears streamed down her face. She experienced a Knowing—our dad was communicating with her. This was not a random thought on Saje's part. Instead, she believes he spoke those words to comfort her. It had been almost a week since Dad had left his physical body, and she missed him immensely. The word *miss* does not even begin to convey what she felt; she yearned for him. However, these moments of connection and signs, this Knowing coming to her in her thoughts, were the beginning of a new kind of comfort for her. She realized that she could build a new type of relationship with our dad, and it was up to her to be open to it.

PADDLE OUT

When our mom brought back our dad's remains from the crematorium, we each took a moment to hold his ashes in the little bag that they came in and shared a mutual Knowing that Dad was more than his ashes, more than the body that had held his soul. Still, even that Knowing did not make the fact that his body wasn't here an easier concept to process.

We decided we would do a paddle out—a Hawaiian ceremony in which mourners paddle out into the ocean on surfboards or paddleboards and sit in a circle taking turns telling stories and honoring the person who has passed before sprinkling their ashes or flowers or mementos into the ocean. Our brother Sands is a surfer, and doing this ritual was particularly important for him. He set about covering one of his boards with flowers and candles, and then we all drove out to Honolua Bay with Mom, Tracy, Shane, Skye, Serena, Sands, Saje, Matt, and Sailor. We chose Honolua Bay because it's a sacred and protected bay on Maui that is frequented by dolphins and turtles, and it's absolutely stunningly beautiful. When we were growing up, our dad took us there countless times for snorkeling and swimming.

Serena's husband, Matt, had to stay on the beach with their daughter Sailor because she was too small to sit on a surfboard, so he snapped a bunch of photos as the rest of us glided into the sea, keeping a surfboard covered in flowers and candles between us. When we were about fifty feet from shore in the middle of the bay, we held hands and took turns speaking to our dad, husband, and friend and asked him to give us a sign that he was with us. Sands's voice broke while he was talking to our dad, and tears streamed down Serena's face.

We recited a few of Dad's favorite poems as well as lines from Herman Melville's *Moby Dick*: "For as this appalling ocean surrounds the verdant land, so in the soul of man there lies one insular Tahiti, full of peace and joy, but encompassed by all the horrors of the half-known life."[1] Our dad always quoted this when he spoke about the importance of living out our dharma of not dying with our own music still in us, so it seemed particularly appropriate to recite that passage while floating on the ocean in a place he loved.

After we sprinkled his ashes into the waves, we spent a few minutes in silence to process it all, and then, with the sun setting behind us, we began to float to the shore. We had asked our dad for a sign while we were out there, but no dolphins jumped around, and not even a feather fell from the sky. Basically, nothing out of the ordinary happened, so it didn't really feel as if we got the sign we were hoping for, which was disappointing.

Serena reached the beach and realized that Saje wasn't with them. She'd paddled even farther out into the ocean and was staring off at the sky. She was always the one who wanted our dad to hold her when we were little, to play with her. Saje was particularly close to him as a baby, way more than Serena ever was, and in that moment of watching her sister paddle out, it was like she was a child again, waiting for her daddy to come home. There she was, his youngest, now an adult of twenty-five but forever his baby wanting her father. This broke Serena's heart into a thousand pieces, and she suffered the enormity of her loss more in that moment than any other up until that point.

Once Saje made her way back to the shore, we piled into our cars to head home and get ready for a celebratory dinner in Dad's honor. Matt started texting Serena all the photos he had taken, as he was riding in a car with our brothers while she was in the car with our mom and sisters. She scrolled through them and stopped, staring at one photo that very clearly had a face shining from the water. She screamed "Holy shit!" Our sisters and mom kept asking "What?" Serena showed them the picture. "You guys, there is a face in the photo right where we paddled out and it is *so* visible, you don't have to squint to see it—it's clear as day!"

Serena sent the photo to everyone in the family and to some of our dad's closest friends as well. Everyone marveled at the fact that this face, which some people even think looks like our dad, showed up in the photo taken during our paddle out while we were asking Dad for a sign. It makes us laugh to think of him enjoying his great cosmic joke and saying, "Oh, you guys want a turtle or dolphin to show up, and that is going to be your sign from me? I can do better than that. How about I put a human face in your photograph? Forget the turtle." Humor was very important in how he interacted with the world. He was so good, so full of love, and he shared those virtues in ways that never brought attention to himself.

RECEIVING AND RETURNING

During these early days, we were constantly reflecting on who our dad was, collecting stories that captured his essence or funny moments we had shared with him. "Unique" doesn't even begin to describe him. One summer, we all put a few photographs of our family on the door of a cabinet in the kitchen in the condo in Maui. When we came back the following summer, the collage of pictures covered *all* the cabinets. The next Christmas, when we were all there, the photos had spread out to the walls! But the best part about this was that about a third of the photos were of people we didn't even know. We would ask, "Dad, who is this kid?" And he would reply, "I have no idea. His mom sent me his picture, so I put it on the wall." Eventually, the condo was pretty much covered with photos of our family and friends and complete strangers, making Dad's love for people always apparent.

Every time we took a walk together on Maui, which was often every day we were there, someone would stop Dad to tell him that his work changed their life, and every time, he would engage with them as if they were the most important person in the world to him. Then he would ask what hotel they were staying in and what their room number was, and he would send one of us kids to deliver a few signed books to their room. This happened constantly—daily, really.

He had an incredibly powerful platform. He drew huge audiences everywhere he went in the world, and he knew how much sharing the stage with him could impact someone's career. Every year, without fail, he would find someone whose cause or story or message he believed in and include them in his program. People like Dan Caro, who became a world-class drummer despite having lost most of his fingers in a fire when he was a little boy. Or Immaculée Ilibagiza, who survived the Rwandan genocide and forgave the people who hunted her and massacred her family and community. Or Anita Moorjani, who, after a near-death experience and healing from cancer, taught others about the importance of self-love. Dad would endorse their work, and if they published something with him, he gave them every dollar of the royalties he collected, never taking any of it for himself.

Dad had an inherent sense of doing what was right, even when it might have been easier to ignore something or take the easier road. He was deeply interested in the world and in people, and this was best reflected by how he modeled generosity. There were many, many stories of his unstinting bigheartedness. Like when he watched a documentary on HBO that highlighted the story of an elderly woman named Harriet Cleveland, who was sixty-one years old, living in Montgomery, Alabama, and raising her three-year-old disabled grandson. Having to choose between paying a fine because she could not afford to renew her car insurance or buying medicine and food, she put the summons in a pile of unpaid bills to attend to later. Over time, the fines accrued interest, eventually going from $75 to more than $4,000. Harriet was arrested in her home in front of her grandson and taken to jail, where she spent two weeks in a cell, awaiting sentencing. Our dad was so moved by her story that he had Dee locate her. When she found Harriet, he wrote her a letter and sent her $4,000 to cover the fine and followed that up with two checks for several thousand dollars to make sure she was all right. Harriet called Dad in tears; she couldn't believe that a complete stranger had sent her more money than she had ever had at one time in her life. This woman's story aired on national television, and only one person—*one person in the whole world*—reached out to help her, without fanfare or praise, and that one person was our dad.

She wasn't the only one. Dad received hundreds of letters each week, and many of them were requests for financial help. Coincidentally, other fans sent him money—people who believed in tithing would send him odd dollar amounts. He put the requests in a pile, and when he received a gift of cash, he sent it to one of the people who had made a request. He maintained a constant flow of financial support to complete strangers just because he could. He paid for college for more than a dozen people unrelated to him, children of friends or even strangers, because he believed in the value of a good education and could provide one. He set up a million-dollar fund at Wayne State University, his alma mater in Detroit, for inner-city kids struggling to pay for school. He'd received breaks from the universe, and he wanted to pass them on. We learned not only the power of receiving from the universe but also the Knowing found in giving back to it.

LOVE LETTERS

When Serena was a teenager, her best friend, Lauren, would come to Maui with our family every summer. Lauren and Serena were in charge of grocery shopping and cooking, and our dad gave them a bank envelope with money in it. Lauren would make our dad laugh, talking about how exciting it was to buy "rich people food" like fresh berries and fish and how great it was to have access to money to buy whatever we wanted at the grocery store for everyone. The one thing Serena kept from our condo on Maui was that bank envelope, the one we had used for more than a decade for the grocery money, because it poignantly reminded her of our dad's generosity, his love of her cooking, and his devotion to his family all at once. She keeps that envelope in her kitchen in Florida and periodically smells it to be reminded of all those carefree days that she spent at the grocery store, blissfully unaware that one day she would be here, unable to fathom that all of that was over.

As Serena put it when she spoke at our dad's celebration of life:

> It is impossible to imagine that you spend so much of your life knowing someone, loving someone, and then in an instant, they are gone, forever. Even though we really believe that the soul goes on, that we live again, it will never be as it was. That is what we spent so much time longing for: what it was. The notion that we are here one minute and gone the next is mind-boggling and terror inducing, and yet it can also provide great

peace. We take odd comfort in the fact that every single person who was on earth 120 years ago is no longer here. That everyone dies, and we all lose people we love, but the world keeps turning, the sun keeps rising, and we continue to have more children, and they can do it all over again. Everyone that once lived has surely experienced loss in this way, and the fact that our experience is not ours alone makes us feel like we belong to a sacred club of people who have lost someone they loved.

We have had friends who have lost someone express doubt over our experience with Dad's passing since they have not had any signs or messages or even dreams about their own loved one who passed away. We cannot speak for anyone else's experience but can say that we believe that every talk our dad gave, every lesson he taught was preparing us and our siblings for this time in our lives. Growing up, we were never made to believe that this was impossible, so for us, it never was. Once again, it comes back to "if you believe it, you'll see it." Perhaps we have experienced Dad in this way because we expected to. And in that same vein, perhaps our friends did not experience their loved ones in this way because they did not expect to. For us, experiencing grief and then learning to dance in the rain is a required part of life. Of growing up. And we are grateful for this Knowing.

Our dad has been the single biggest force of love and joy we have ever encountered. He always looked within himself for change, even when situations were tough, rather than looking outside of himself and expecting the conditions that were making life tough to change for him. He never compromised on his dharma—he came here with a purpose, and he never allowed anything to get in the way of his ultimate calling. We find that so inspiring. He loved us, and we felt his love every moment we were together, every time we spoke, even every time we screwed up. We really, really, really felt his love, and that has always been the best feeling in the world for us.

A Way of Knowing

When we experience joy,
we experience God.

Our dad's voicemail for at least the last ten years he was alive went like this: "Hi, this is Wayne Dyer that you've reached, and I want to feel good. So if your message is designed to do anything other than this, you've reached the wrong number and perhaps you should call Dr. Phil." This is a silly example, but it's something he wholeheartedly believed in.

Feeling good is feeling God, and it's when we are vibrating at the high-level energy of joy that we attract more joy. It's easy to say, but what do you do when you're not feeling good? When you can't see the stars in daylight? For us, it starts with forgiving yourself, not judging yourself for whatever you're feeling, and then reaching for the best emotion you can manage at that time—joyous, delighted, or perhaps just okay. It is not realistic to skip right to joy, but try for anything that elevates, because a step up is progress.

This reminds us of the often-quoted and shared lines from author and spiritual intuitive Esther Hicks: "The only thing that makes the difference in the way you feel right now is the thought that you are thinking right now. It doesn't matter how much money you've got; there are joyful people with no money, and there are unhappy people with lots of money. How you feel is about how you are allowing the Source that is You to flow . . . we're talking about the art of living; about the art of thriving; about the art of clarity. We're talking about the art of being who you really are."[2]

You can choose to live from that place of recognizing that the universe is responding to you and guiding you and supporting you and inspiring you. Then you can look at how you feel when those things come up and recognize that when you feel joy, you feel in alignment, you feel inspired, and you feel like you're on your path. That's the key to the Knowing. Are you heading in the direction you want to go or not?

One of the best ways to find that direction is to connect to the person you really are. To cultivate feeling good and high vibration is to do things that bring you joy by bringing joy to someone else. We have found that when you really take a close look, feeling good for others' happiness very often feels even better than feeling good for yourself. Try being of service to others, offering compliments or a "dad joke" or a random kindness, or maybe tell someone you really, really, really love them.

Saje recalls something Dad explained to her as she was growing up that struck her in a way she never forgot. Our dad was an avid tennis player, and for years he played on a daily basis. One day he was talking about how there were times in his games when he became so energetically aligned with the game that *everything* just went right for him. The ball stayed inside the lines by a millimeter, he was always in the right spot at the right time, and the game just continuously went his way. He talked about how *good* it feels when you are in this kind of energetic alignment, how you almost feel invincible, and with each move you make, you just know it's going your way.

But then he talked about how there are times when your opponent gets into one of these grooves, and no matter how hard you try, everything just keeps going right for *them*. He explained that he would often become frustrated when this happened but that frustration just seemed to cause him to play worse and his opponent to play better. Until one day he experimented with feeling genuine joy and happiness for his opponent when they were "in the groove."

And what happened then? This genuine joy that he felt for another person's success catapulted him right back into his own groove, and he would end up playing some of the best competitive tennis of his life. Being happy for others' happiness just brings about more happiness. When you find yourself unable to muster happy feelings about anything that is going on for you, work on feeling them for someone else, and just watch how you shift back into energetic alignment.

So how can you muster these feelings of joy for others when you aren't organically feeling them already? One way is to repeat a mantra. Mantras can work miracles at shifting the direction your thoughts are heading. If you find yourself in a situation similar to the example of our dad playing tennis, in which you are desiring someone else to fail, you will probably notice that you continue to feel worse energetically, and nothing changes about the other person's behavior. In order to shift this, try saying to yourself, "I feel genuine happiness for the success of others." Repeat this in your mind until it's true, and we guarantee this will shift you back into a place of feeling good. Another mantra that we love is "Joy is right here now." These simple little words can serve as a powerful reminder that joy is not attached to a destination or a goal but instead is readily available to you at all times. It's just up to you to tune in.

When we were children, our dad traveled a lot for work. Sometimes he would come home with a gift for Saje, sometimes with one for Sommer or Shane, and if any of us made a comment like "Why didn't you get me something?" he would always respond that with eight children, he could either pick up something for one of us when he saw something that reminded him of that particular child, or he could come home with nothing, but there was no way he could pick out eight individual gifts every time he traveled just for the sake of making it "fair." He would often say to us as children, "You should be happy for your brother or sister that they got a special gift, and they should be happy for you when it is your time to get a special gift." We heard this so often that by the time we were teenagers we were genuinely happy for each other whenever one of us got a special gift from our parents.

It took a little growing up for us to really understand the concept of feeling genuine happiness for someone else getting a gift or achieving a level of success or accomplishing a major goal. But because we were taught from a young age not to make it always about ourselves, we really did learn to genuinely support each other and be happy for each other when things worked out for one of us, so there was never a sense of needing to compete for attention or fight over things being "fair."

For Serena, as a parent to three children all close in age, this can be hard to demonstrate at times, and one could argue that it is easier to pull off when you have as many children as our parents did. But even now, Serena finds herself repeating those same words to her own children: "You should be happy for your sister that she got a special gift, and when you get a special gift, she should be happy for you too." Getting your children to support one another from an early age can be easily taught, and over time, it can become their automatic response.

CHAPTER 6

Choosing Sooner

"Your trust in this inner knowing is all you need.
I call it faith—not faith in an external god to
provide you with a purpose, but faith in the call
you're hearing from the center of your being."

DR. WAYNE W. DYER,
THE POWER OF INTENTION

"CALL DAD"

Growing up around our dad's teachings, Saje was both a skeptic *and* a believer. Sometimes she thought the things he talked about were a little airy-fairy—especially when it came to death and dying and the soul, perhaps because they didn't apply to her experience. When Dad died, she felt challenged in a new way. Was she going to be a person of logic who says, "I can't see you, I can't feel you, I can't hear you; you're gone"? Or was she going to see the stars in daylight, to dig a little deeper and find the divine part of herself—the Knowing—to take his teachings and apply them to her life? As she came to accept that our dad is still with us all the time and paid attention to the signs around her, she studied his work in a whole new light and reached a turning point. She became a more spiritual person committed to the truth that we might seem limited to our physical body and sensory input, seeing there is more to it than that. And still, Saje struggled.

In the weeks and months after my dad left his physical body, I held on to ideas about how things should be, and I wholeheartedly resisted the idea that he was physically gone. Even if I wasn't doing this consciously, I was certainly doing it subconsciously. I can't even begin to tell you the number of dreams that I had where I would find my dad and be overjoyed and relieved that he was still alive. Or dreams where I would try to convince my dad that he did not have to die. Or dreams where I found a way to "bring him back" into his physical body. The list goes on and on, but the theme in all of these dreams was that I was resisting, with every fiber of my being, this idea that he was gone from the way that I was used to experiencing him. I was resisting the idea that he was gone from the physical world. I was clinging to what was familiar and comfortable, which for me and for most of us is having our loved ones here with us, experiencing life in the same way we are, never more than a phone call away, with a physical smell, a body to clothe and feed—someone to be physically present with.

When I was lost in the whirlwind of grief, attempting to process my loss and make it something I could control and fix, I would find myself returning to thoughts of "Call Dad—he will make this better" or "When you see Dad again, it will all be fine," only to realize over and over again that these were no longer options. I could not call my dad or see my dad or talk with him. I could not control this or box it up into a nice little package and have it make sense the way most of the other things in my life up until this point had made sense.

I have no judgment around this. I think it is natural to have these reactions and dreams and thoughts. I see no point in creating judgment around any feelings or thoughts you have while in the throes of grief. Feel what you feel and experience what you experience, but try to take time to be the observer to all of this. Once I started to observe the ways in which I was going through the motions and to observe the types of thoughts swirling through my mind, I began to realize that many of these ideas and dreams were fear based. They arose out of the fear I have of death, of loss, and of the unknown. They also came from a place of trying to find some control, which, after all, is also a fear-based desire. When you cling to something, you are basically saying to the universe, "I don't really have this, because if I don't hold on tight, it will be gone."

What Saje began to notice after making the conscious decision to become the observer is that our fear of a situation is created by our thoughts about that situation, which brings us back to "If you change the way you look at things, the things you look at change." What's remarkable is it's not just a psychological or spiritual truth, it's a scientific one as well. In physics, there's something called "the observer effect," which states, "The observation of a phenomenon changes that phenomenon." Studies have shown that even passive observation of quantum phenomena—the smallest scale of energy levels and atomic particles—can change the measured result.

It's important to note that this isn't mind control—it's not conscious but instead energetic. In other words, the energy an observer brings to the observation has an impact on the way particles behave. Everything is energy. When you shift how you look at all the things that happen in your life, the energy of your life shifts as well. When you stay committed to thoughts of lack, fear, doubt, and dread, you stay connected to those thoughts, and your life *becomes* one of lack, fear, doubt, and dread. When you choose thoughts in harmony with what you would like to happen in your life—hope, peace, and surrender—you are vibrating at a different energetic frequency, and as a result, you open up that path of least resistance, aligning with what you seek. We've come to call this "choosing sooner."

To grow from this, to experience our dad in a new way, and to be open to his signs and encouragement, Saje understood she had to surrender to the situation she was in. She had to surrender to love and to the Knowing that she was still cared for and would be okay without our dad here in his physical body, even if she couldn't see how yet.

The surrender she began to practice and continues to practice is exactly that—a practice. It's not a decision she made and then never looked back. It's something she reminds herself to do daily. When she catches herself trying to control a situation, especially one that is impossible to control, she stops and tries to empty her mind of the spiderweb of thoughts she's created. Once it feels clear, or at least a little bit slowed down, she says this silent prayer of surrender: "Dear God, I am ready to see this in a new way." Through this, she can take the path of least resistance.

When you cling to something or even someone, you are saying to the universe, "I don't really have this, because if I don't hold on tight, it will be gone." Clinging is the opposite of allowing. You can spend your entire life clinging to control and to the way you think things ought to be, or you can let go and trust the nature of the universe at play. If you spend your life attached to the belief that things should fall into place the way you think they ought to, you'll spend your whole life swimming against the flow of the universe, traveling the path of most resistance. When you live a life based in faith instead of fear, when you surrender, the universe will support you, and you will attract more of that allowing.

Fear cannot exist where love is overwhelming, and surrendering to the Knowing that all is in divine order is the same as surrendering to love. It creates the space for love to enter, for the miracles to appear, and for you to grow as a person (which is what we are all on earth to do).

Hardships and death are a part of life. They crack us open to allow the light in, to find meaning in loss, to grow, and to help others. Saje came to see that in a time-less universe, "forever" and "never" do not exist. We all come here with a round-trip ticket. Therefore, we know with certainty we will someday join our departed loved ones in the realm where they are now. She began to rec-ognize our dad still exists in her life.

THERE'S NO SCHEDULE FOR SORROW

Our dad often lectured about the beauty of death, describ-ing it as a world of infinite love. One of the stories he often told was about a father whose son, a soldier, died in war. The night after receiving the news, the father went out dancing, and someone asked, "How could you do this? How could you possibly be out dancing when you've just learned that your son has died?" The man replied, "At some point, I'm going to have to move on from my sorrow, or it's going to kill me. I'm just choosing sooner." There's no rule for how long you must stay stuck in any problem in life. There's no schedule for disappointment or righteous indignation, fear, or grief.

Recalling this story gave Saje the boost she needed. She could choose sooner. There was no prescribed amount of time that she had to be stuck. Our dad often said, "You are only stuck if you choose to be," and Saje could choose to start seeing the miracles. This, of course, didn't mean her sadness disappeared. And it also didn't mean that experi-encing the grief as sadness was bad—it's important to cry those tears and feel however it is you are feeling! It just helped her realize that she didn't need permission to start being happy even as she was grieving his loss. Choosing "sooner" shifted her perspective on death in general and opened her up to start receiving signs and miracles and to become the student of her situation instead of the victim.

Saje experienced the Knowing in her own way after the celebration of our dad's life when she was back in New York. She faced the decision of returning to graduate school or taking some time off. No one would fault her for taking a break, since she'd been through so much in the past weeks. The dean of her university was generous and offered her the opportunity to take a leave of absence with no academic repercussions. Saje considered this—she was still grieving. She had to decide whether she was ready to be back at school only a couple of weeks after our dad had made his transition. This decision turned out to be easy. Because of dad's insistence that she accept the money that would enable her to finish school, she knew there was only one place that she should be: back at school, learning psychology, and following his footsteps into the counseling world.

We are certain that Dad had a Knowing that his time was coming. He was generous, an innate provider. This was his nature. We firmly believe that our dad's time to be called back came in divine time, and the higher part of him that sensed this knew he could never leave this earth without fulfilling his promise to put Saje through graduate school. She could finish her degree at NYU because our dad had listened to his inner voice; now it was time for us to listen to ours. It was a lesson he taught us in many different ways: always listen to the soft inner nudgings of your soul, even when the loud voice of your ego does all it can to overpower them. One way we have found to distinguish between the two is to simply ask which choice is coming from love.

DON'T FEAST ON FEAR

When Serena's water broke at five in the morning on March 30, 2015, the first person she called—even before waking up Matt or texting our mom to meet her at the hospital—was our dad, even though he was on Maui and she was in Florida. She wanted to hear his voice first, because she knew the next hours would be busy, to say the least. After a long and painful twenty hours of labor, Sailor Marcelene entered the world and captured the hearts of her entire family from minute one.

From the day they brought their beautiful little baby Sailor home from the hospital, Serena's husband, Matt, was involved and supportive, but Serena was stressed out and exhausted nonetheless. She experienced a mix of fear, anxiety, and depression over the complete lack of sleep and general sense that she was somehow not capable of taking care of a small baby. She also had about thirty pounds to lose from her pregnancy and felt consumed by needing to feel good about her body. Looking back, Serena thinks she lost sight of the fact that she gave birth to a healthy and beautiful baby girl and instead focused her attention on the lack of freedom and sleep that came with her arrival. From where she is now in life—four years later and with three kids under five years old—it seems laughable that Serena would stress about something like losing weight or not getting enough sleep. At the time, she didn't think things could get worse. But they did.

When Sailor was two months old, Serena woke up from a rare night's sleep at around seven in the morning to feed the baby. She was in good spirits—she was getting the hang of this mothering thing and excited because she and Matt and their daughter were going to Key West the following day with a bunch of friends and family for Serena's thirtieth birthday celebration.

As Sailor was nursing, Serena heard a thunderous pounding. It sounded like an army was trying to kick their front door down! Still dressed in her nightgown and holding her newborn in her arms, she ran to the door and opened it. About a dozen police officers were on the other side, guns drawn and wielding a battering ram! She screamed as they pushed past her and asked if Matt was at home. They exploded into her house to find her husband, who had been awoken by the commotion, standing in his underwear, completely confused. Almost immediately, they took him away, and Serena was left holding her hungry baby, wondering what the hell had happened. Sailor started screaming, and Serena tried to feed her to comfort her, but she was unable to latch onto Serena's breast no matter how hard she tried, probably because she was picking up on her mother's stress.

Serena ran upstairs, called Matt's attorney, and felt her heart hammering through her chest. She decided she wasn't going to tell anyone what had happened, assuming this was an awful mistake. So she called a babysitter, who came over immediately, and got dressed to go meet with her husband's attorney and arrange his release. Serena wondered if Matt was going to be out in time to go to Key West, since they had been looking forward to it, and she didn't want to miss her own party. She was clueless.

As she was getting ready to walk out the door, the doorbell rang. Serena looked out the window and saw a news van parked outside the house and a reporter and cameraperson standing at her front door. Serena still had no idea what was going on, but she realized that she needed to let her family know what was happening.

Serena called Saje, who was in Montreal with Dad, and Saje flew to Florida the next day. Our dad was committed to teaching in Canada, so Serena FaceTimed him and felt immediate relief when he answered and smiled at her, asking her how Sailor was. Serena told him the police had arrested Matt and that CBS News was outside her house, asking for a comment. Our dad asked, "Is he dealing drugs?" and for some reason, this made Serena laugh out loud.

Matt was not dealing drugs. Once she connected with the lawyer, she learned that Matt's business had been shut down and was being investigated for mail fraud and a variety of other charges, all of which seemed like government overreach. Nonetheless, they were criminal charges, and suddenly Matt's life, his freedom, and their family's livelihood were on the line. His charges, if he was convicted, carried a prison term of decades. *Decades.*

Matt had once had a newsletter business that mailed out marketing pieces (junk mail) designed to get people excited about winning sweepstakes. These were sent all over the world, and people who were interested in potentially winning—mostly "sweepers" or gamblers—would send twenty dollars in exchange for a comprehensive report on upcoming sweepstakes and prize giveaways. These reports were compiled by a staff of people, taking the legwork out of it for the consumer. There is a world-wide industry based around these kinds of offers. Any time a consumer complained or was dissatisfied with Matt's company's newsletter, they received a full refund, no questions asked. Serena and Matt did not believe that his business was illegal, but it was not up to them, so his indictment stood. The timing of all of this seemed particularly odd, since Matt had stopped working in the sweepstakes industry before he and Serena were married, so she couldn't understand why the police were arresting him for a business he hadn't been involved in for years.

Nine hours after the police burst into Serena's home, Sands and our mom accompanied Serena to Florida District Court, where they watched as Matt stood in shackles. As they entered the courtroom, the bailiff advised them not to make eye contact with the "prisoner" because if it seemed they were trying to signal some sort of message, they would be escorted out. Serena, our mom, and Sands listened as the judge agreed to release Matt on bond if certain conditions were met. The most difficult condition was that they needed assurance in the form of property worth a significant amount of money that was owned outright by someone who was willing to put a lien against it in order to guarantee that if her husband "made a run for it," the house could be seized.

Serena kept thinking how impossible that seemed, to find someone willing to do that within a twenty-four-hour period. Our dad was not comfortable with the idea of putting up the family's Boca house for his release, but our mom went against his wishes and did it anyway. She signed over the deed of their house to guarantee Matt's release, and while she signed the paperwork, she told jokes and acted silly to distract Serena, which made the whole experience even more sad, painful, and beautiful at the same time.

> The love, the protectiveness, the kindness I felt from her was so pure in that moment that it reminded me of this concept of *Shibumi*, the Japanese word for the idea of something being so simple, so subtle, and so beautiful that you can't put it into words. My mom trying to make light of what she was doing to protect me from more stress than I was already feeling was one of the single most beautiful moments of my entire life. It fully taught me everything it means to be a mother and serve your children. Her graciousness at the courthouse was one of many moments like that, which I would experience from her in the years to come. The pain I felt in having to watch her risk her home for my husband and me, coupled with the humility I was experiencing—since at this point, the arrest was public knowledge—mixed with the gratitude I had in who she had revealed herself to be in my darkest moment was so poignant and real that I can still feel it as I write this.

Serena's husband was released from prison to await trial two days before her thirtieth birthday. The celebration he had spent months planning for twenty or so of their friends and family members in the Keys still happened, but she and Matt weren't there for it. The night of the party was the night Matt was released from prison, and Serena will never forget the feeling she had when he walked in their front door after his attorney dropped him off. He was wearing his prison uniform and shoes, and he collapsed into her arms, sobbing and telling her again and again how much he loved her and how grateful he was to have her. The tenderness Serena felt for him in that moment, her Knowing that she would always stand by his side, no matter what, and be strong for him as he fought this legal battle, became even more clear for her as she held him. After witnessing our parents' decision to stay connected in love and trust, even after choosing to go in different directions in their personal lives, Serena realized that you can always write the story of your life on your own terms, and she knew that she would always stay by Matt's side, no matter what legal issues were to come. Real love, she had learned as a teenager years before, was accepting someone for who they were, without conditions.

FEED FAITH

Three months after Matt's arrest, our dad passed away. In the months that followed, Serena tried to resume her "regular" life, but everything seemed amplified, especially her love for her baby daughter Sailor and the stress of Matt's legal troubles. She wished she could share her worries with our dad like she used to. Throughout the process of Matt's legal battle, the fear that they might lose their home, their savings, and their dreams became all-consuming. Whenever any little thing happened, like an update from an attorney, Serena would call everybody she knew and talk about it with them and analyze it and obsess over what it might mean. It became overwhelming. For many of those years leading up to and after the trial, she chose to resist life as it unfolded, but then something shifted—she asked herself: *Is the fear of experiencing life without Dad, of losing our home, of my husband going to prison serving me?* When she connected to her expanding Knowing, she realized the answer.

Serena recalled something Dad had said to her after the arrest and soon before he died. "Do not talk about this constantly. Do not obsess over it. Don't feast on it all day every day. All you are doing is feeding more energy into the problem that you don't want to have. If you need to talk about it, do, and then let go and let God. Do not become obsessed over every little thing that happens along the way. Just trust that the ultimate bigger picture, the outcome is in your highest good. Know that, and God will handle the rest."

She realized all she was doing was feeding into the energy of what she didn't want. Ultimately, she had to just trust that everything would work out, even if it didn't happen as fast as or in the way that she wanted it to happen. She had to surrender to the experience and trust that it was all in divine order even though it seemed bad. She had to accept that she was placing a judgment on what she was experiencing by labeling it as bad but that ultimately every experience is something that leads to growth.

The way to do this in matters large or small is to become a student of circumstance, not the victim. One of the ways to do this is to stop, be quiet for a moment, and weigh the scale of the problem. Is it worth melting down over the slow internet service? If you're five minutes late to your meeting, will anything bad really happen? And on a bigger scale, how can you begin to heal from anger and pain if you remain in a state of anger and pain?

At a conference hosted by Oprah Winfrey, Serena heard a guest of Oprah's, Jesse Israel, speak. Jesse founded The Big Quiet, a movement that facilitates large groups of people across the country meditating together. Jesse explained that when we were hunters and gatherers, we developed the fight-or-flight response in order to deal with real-life predators like saber-toothed tigers while we were out foraging for food. He explained that when the flight-or-fight response kicks in, our reproductive and digestive systems immediately shut off to preserve energy; our blood thickens so that, in the event of an attack, we have less risk of bleeding out; and our heart and breathing rates and blood pressure increase due to the release of adrenaline, which helps us fight or flee. This physiological response takes about an hour to dissipate after the initial encounter. Jesse went on to explain that in our modern world, in which we are constantly bombarded by triggers, from stressful meetings to

After that moment of Knowing, in each situation she faced, she really had to ask, "Do I want to be a hostage to the thoughts and associations and beliefs and fears and dread of what people might think or what the outcome might be?" She would find herself thinking, "Am I not worthy of what I have or of attracting a good life?" Eventually, she realized that those are all thoughts designed by the ego. The alternative to that is to say, "I choose, in each difficult situation that I find myself in, to find the meaning in the experience. In doing so, I allow myself to move closer to God, spirit, and my higher self and to view each experience as an opportunity to grow." When we cannot change the circumstances of our lives, we can change how we respond to them, how we view them, and how we evolve. Through the process of losing our father, we saw we had a choice: to become defined by loss, to be held back, or to be transformed by infinite love, to reach the Knowing.

OUT OF THE DEPTHS

The biggest gift that occurred for Serena during the entirety of her husband's legal turmoil was in watching him transform into a man who was able to send love toward the very people prosecuting him. When he found out one of his co-defendants had flipped against him, he never once expressed ill will toward the man and instead focused on sending him love and compassion. The experience of this legal process opened her up to a new way of thinking, living, and being. Matt, instead of viewing himself as a victim of an unfair legal system, chose instead to see all of this as a gift.

He expressed to Serena that he now views his entire ordeal as an experience that he signed up for long before he incarnated in this lifetime, and he says that he trusts he chose this experience for his soul to grow. After all, we come here to learn, to grow, and to offer those lessons to others, and then we return to the place from which we came. If we are lucky, when we get to the end of our lives, we will look back and see that we have spent our lives growing in the direction of love. Serena believes she and Matt both needed this experience to remind them that love and service, not financial success and ego-based accomplishments, make up the basis for our existence. She believes that most people will live their lives without ever experiencing the circumstances that make us ask ourselves, "Am I truly worthy of these teachings? And can I stay awake enough while alive to get this lesson and then use it to help others?"

Serena has come to a place in her life where she is able to contemplate any difficult situation she finds herself in and view it not as a punishment or a curse but rather as a gift that she signed up to experience in order to allow her soul to grow in the biggest and most beautiful way possible. As Roy and Jane Nichols wrote, "The most beautiful people we have known are those who have known defeat, known suffering, known struggle, known loss, and have found their way out of the depths. These persons have an appreciation, a sensitivity, and an understanding of life that fills them with compassion, gentleness, and a deep loving concern. Beautiful people do not just happen."[1]

We believe that shifting our perspective, in any difficult situation, toward "What is this teaching me?" opens up the space for us to take the first step in experiencing the miracle that this situation has to offer. Choosing to focus not on "Why me?" but instead on "How may I use this to serve?" allows us to experience the miracle that awaits us when we shift our perception and "choose sooner."

A Way of Knowing

Be the student of your circumstances, not the victim.

Of course it's okay and necessary to feel what you are feeling when tragedies or troubles arise, but also know that "choosing sooner" is always an option. You can take the necessary steps to avoid becoming a victim of your circumstances. Even in our everyday lives, when things are going well, we can choose sooner. For example, if someone makes you angry or you've had your fill of rush-hour traffic or whiny children, staying in a mind of annoyance only troubles *you*, so make an effort to choose joy sooner. When you're disappointed that you didn't get what you were hoping for—a sunny day or landing a job after a great interview—you can still choose joy and choose it sooner. Let the lost job become an opportunity to finally finish your degree. Let the burnt dinner be a reason to have an impromptu pizza party with your kids.

getting cut off in traffic to mailboxes full of over-due bills, our bodies respond to these as dangers.

On a physiological level, we have not yet evolved to distinguish between an antagonistic email from a coworker and a saber-toothed tiger looking at us as its next meal. What this means for each of us is that we are constantly experiencing physiological effects even when our survival is not being threatened. In order to counter this, meditation and turning off the "noise" allow our bodies to respond to the non–life-threatening threats we experience more adequately, and in doing so, we actually become healthier, calmer, and more capable human beings.

Looking back, Serena could see how she was often responding to every little thing that came up during the legal battle from a place of fear, which was causing her flight-or-fight response to be triggered multiple times a day, every day, for weeks on end. When she got to the place at which she really could reflect on her father's words of not allowing every little thing to have an impact and to trust in the process, she was able to find more peace in each day. As we have all heard many times but always need to hear again, life is not defined by what happens to you. Instead, it is defined by how you choose to respond to the events that are unfolding that are out of your control. In every situation, as our dad used to say, "You can choose peace rather than this." And you can choose it sooner.

CHAPTER 7

Take Your Shoes Off

"I know that even in the most troublesome of
times my reaction is to choose stillness."

Dr. Wayne W. Dyer,
*Change Your Thoughts
—Change Your Life*

THE GENERAL CONSECRATION
OF THE UNIVERSE

We all need stillness in our lives if we want to get closer to
our intuition and to the Knowing, and we need to make a
point to incorporate that silence into our days no matter
what our schedule holds—no matter how many emails
need to be answered or how many times a phone buzzes.
Trust us, we both have seven chatty siblings, and our texts
about the most mundane things seem to go on all day!

When we were growing up, our mom modeled a dedication to meditation. She meditated every single day, for
at least twenty minutes, without ever missing a day. She
usually did this in her bedroom, with her sign on the
door, but we can also remember times when getting

twenty minutes to herself just seemed impossible with a house full of kids, soccer practice, music lessons, doctors' appointments, and the inherent chaos of mothering a pack of little humans. On those days, she still didn't miss her meditation! Sometimes it meant that we had to be quiet for twenty minutes in the backseat of the family van while we waited for our sister Skye to finish her singing lessons. Other times, it meant that during a school event, Mom went to the back of the bleachers where no one was nearby and sat in silence. No matter what, she always fed her mind with this silence, and now that we are older, it is truly inspiring to see the impact of this dedication. Our mother is always calm. Between us, we can count on one hand the number of times we have witnessed her lose her cool. Nothing rattles her, and she is always tuned in to her Knowing. Not to mention she looks half her age and has never been seriously ill!

It wasn't until Saje was a little older, however, that she took an interest in meditation. When she was twenty-one, she was on Maui with Dad, who had recently taken up the Moses Code meditation that James Twyman popularized. Our father was excited about this meditation and told Saje how it could dramatically change her life. She agreed to practice with him every day for the three weeks she was on Maui. He instructed her to begin her mantra with "I am" and follow with whatever she wanted to manifest. Saje had recently suffered her first heartbreak, so she jumped on the opportunity to complete her mantra with "in love," which meant being back in love and in a relationship with her ex. This meditation brought such peace to her mind that by the end of the trip, she had changed her mantra to "I *am* love," realizing that she and we all are love—perfect, whole, and complete with or without a romantic partner. This was Saje's first real introduction to a regular meditation practice. However, she eventually let it go and only did the Moses Code meditation on occasion. It wasn't until after our dad shed his physical body that her interest and need to meditate were reignited.

In the years since we've lost our dad and have come to realize and focus on the idea that there is infinitely more to the universe than our physical bodies are capable of discerning, we've become fascinated with expanding our minds and syncing with the signs of what else is out there. In our own ways, we've become interested in learning how to get closer to God and to be more open to hearing and feeling our loved ones who have passed on—which, if we're being completely honest, was not something we were especially interested in before experiencing profound loss.

This has not been an easy practice, and it takes a great deal of discipline, something we all struggle with, especially when life gets in the way. From working to parenting to just wanting to relax with some Netflix, there are a million excuses to put off meditation. We get it. It can appear that you are accomplishing more if you tackle that list of emails that need to be answered or those dishes piling up in the sink, but we are here to tell you that meditation should be the priority! We have both found that through meditation we feel closer to our dad, to peace, and to the Knowing. We're better moms, we're more patient, and we're far more intuitive.

At this point, you know how much our dad loved to quote Herman Melville, and he often repeated these words that are so pertinent to meditation: "Silence is the general consecration of the universe. . . Silence is the only Voice of our God."[1] In a similar vein, Dad said, "It has been said that it is the space between the bars that holds the tiger. And it's the silence between the notes that makes the music. It is out of silence, or 'the gap,' or that space between our thoughts, that everything is created—including our own bliss."[2]

"I'M GOING FOR A WALK WITH DAD"

When we are disciplined in our meditation practice, we receive more signs from our dad. We are better at hearing our intuition and blocking out all the background chatter. We can see that this life we are living is temporary, as are all the emotions we feel in any given day. When we get bad news, we can stop from spiraling into pessimism and instead stay on the outside and realize that this "bad news" is not who we are, and it is inconsequential in the grand scheme of the universe. We take ourselves a little bit less seriously and can differentiate between who we are as infinite souls and the voice in our heads that has ideas and opinions on everything. Essentially, we are better people when we make an effort to meditate on a regular basis.

For Saje's whole life, she often heard people who had lost someone say things like "I can truly feel the presence of my deceased loved one right now." Our dad often said things like this on stage about his mother or his father or even about various saints and authors who had passed on and whose teachings he had studied—like Saint Francis of Assisi or Lao-tzu. After our dad lost his mom (our grandma), when he was seventy-three years old, he often told Saje about times that he felt his mother's presence, whether in a dream or while going for a walk. When she would hear our dad or anyone talk like this, in all honesty, she would think to herself, "But do you *really*?" She found it hard to believe that you could "feel" the presence of a person who had passed on. How did you feel them? What made you know they were with you?

She's not saying that she didn't believe some people could feel the presence of their loved ones who had left their physical bodies. Admittedly, though, she did find it difficult to believe, mostly because she didn't understand it. Until our dad left his physical body, she had never lost someone who was truly close to her. She was skeptical of this aspect of spirituality. She didn't disbelieve it but had no real reason for believing it. It didn't apply to her.

But then came the day that it began to apply to her in a big way. We all went out to Maui after our first Christmas since Dad had died. Dad's condo had been reopened for the first time, and we needed to get it back in order, not to mention our desire to just be back in his home. Being back in that space made Saje even more desperate to feel his presence and know he was still with her. She thought about the fact that others around her had often expressed that they feel their loved ones who have left this earthly plane and wondered if or when this would happen to her.

When our dad was still alive, he took a walk every day, and whenever he was in Maui, he always traveled the same route: along the beach of Kaanapali down to the Hyatt Hotel, through the Hyatt lobby, over to Canoe Beach, and then back the same way to where he started. He liked to wear tennis shoes for the extra support while he did this walk, so he always stayed on the sidewalk instead of walking on the sand. Whenever Saje was in Maui with our dad, she would join him on this daily walk. It was part of their routine when she was there, and whenever he was getting ready to head out, he would say "Quagey, are you ready for our walk? Come on, let's go!" If there was ever a day that Saje didn't feel like going, our dad wouldn't take no for an answer, and she would inevitably end up doing this walk with him.

So when she was out in Maui in January of 2016, six months after Dad had left his physical body, she decided she was still going to take "his" walk each day. She decided to follow the exact route he always took—down to the Hyatt, through the hotel lobby, onto Canoe Beach, and then turn around and take the same route back, the entire time staying on the sidewalk. She decided she would listen to one of his recorded lectures while she walked.

On the very first day that Saje did this, she hadn't bothered to put on her walking shoes and was wearing some flimsy flip-flops. After walking for about ten minutes, her legs and feet began to ache from the lack of supportive shoes, not to mention it was midday and the sun was blazing. With the combination of sore legs and feet and the hot sun, she was about ready to turn around and commit to going for the walk tomorrow, earlier in the day and wearing the correct shoes. Just as she was about to head back to our condo, she heard our dad's voice in her head: "Take your shoes off, honey."

It reminded her of a poem by Elizabeth Barret Browning that our dad often quoted.

> Earth's crammed with heaven,
> And every common bush afire with God;
> But only he who sees, takes off his shoes . . . [3]

But only he who sees, takes off his shoes . . . Was Saje imagining things? Unsure, she took off her flip-flops and continued to walk on the sidewalk. A minute or so later, she wasn't feeling any more into the walk than she had been with her shoes on and again was about to turn around and head back to the condo when once again, she heard our dad's voice speaking to her, only this time he said, "Now, go walk on the sand." For whatever reason, she decided to listen to this voice again and walked out onto the sand.

As soon as she got down to the wet part of the sand and began walking on the beach, as the cool ocean water splashed on her feet and calves, she immediately felt refreshed. The water on her legs, coupled with the sand massaging her feet, gave her a renewed energy that was unexpected. As she continued walking and listening to our dad's lecture through her headphones, she began to feel like our dad was with her. In fact, she *knew* he was with her. It was as if she was doing the walk with him, as they had always done when he was still here in his body. She can't really explain how she knew he was with her; she felt him and continued walking with a smile on her face. Saje felt like she had a secret—a secret that no one else on that entire beach knew. And she did not want this walk to end.

She felt like she could walk forever if it meant she could stay with this feeling.

When she reached Canoe Beach, which was the point to turn around, she did so because the terrain turns rocky and there is no way to continue in the sand. As she made her way back to the condo, she wasn't ready to stop. She knew she had to be ready to go to dinner shortly, so she told herself she could walk for ten more minutes past our condo before she needed to turn around and go home. And that was what she did. When it was time to turn around, she felt nervous—as though if she stopped walking, the feeling would go away forever. She desperately did not want this walk to come to an end. But then she heard our dad speak again, and this time he said, "It doesn't end here, honey. We walk together always." And in that moment, the tears welled up in her eyes.

The moment she turned around to head home, she looked out into the distance and saw two whales jumping completely out of the ocean and slamming their bodies back down into the water, causing a terrific splash. She smiled. She knew Dad had helped her to see them.

Every single day of that trip, Saje took a walk with our dad. She would even say to our family before setting out, "I'll be back in an hour. I'm going for my walk with Dad." In our family, this seemed completely normal, because we all know in our own ways that our father is still here with us, and we see no reason we can't take a walk with him, even if he isn't here as a physical presence any longer. And each day while she was on that walk, she had that same feeling settle into her. It was almost euphoric. And every single time, she knew without a doubt that our dad was walking beside her. Whenever she returns to Maui now, she takes that walk. It's her time for herself and her time to be with Dad.

Saje knows it's easy to take what she says about hearing our dad's voice and chalk it up to her own mind creating these thoughts. She questioned this herself and sometimes still does. But the reason she knows it wasn't her is because the thought came out of nowhere. She wasn't thinking about our dad in that moment, nor was she imagining a dialogue with him in her mind—she was only thinking about how hot she was and how she was ready to turn around and give up the walk for the day. And then in popped this thought that ended up being exactly what she needed to hear to complete the walk. The other reason she knows it wasn't her own thought is because she would never call herself "honey." Only someone else, specifically our dad, would call her that.

Saje cautions readers that hearing our dad's voice in her mind is not something that happens to her very often. She wishes she could hear our dad's voice in her mind daily, but that's not the case. However, she's paid attention enough to realize that when she does hear Dad, it's when she's calm and rested and when her mind is at peace, and that is when she is regularly practicing meditation. If we want to "hear" and "feel" and "know" our loved ones are still with us, we must invite more silence into our lives. We must quiet our minds to be able to discern between the noise and whispers of God. "If I don't do this," Saje realizes, "the noise of my mind makes it impossible to hear our dad, to hear my intuition, to hear God."

Saje has come to realize that in her life, there is rarely silence. She lives in New York City, so that explains half of it, but aside from all the noise of the city that never sleeps, there is a lot of other noise in her life. She's busy with her baby boy, Julian, which certainly does not add any silence! She's on the phone all the time—we have such a big family, and we're lucky to say that we're so close to everyone in it, but this takes up a lot of free time during the day. When she's not talking to family, she's with friends. She reads a lot, but this still is not silence. Saje and her husband own a restaurant in Manhattan, which means a life of constant social interaction. And lastly, even when her ears aren't detecting any outside noise, her mind is always running. There is nothing wrong with any of these aspects of life, but contemplating them made her realize that if she wanted silence so that she can get closer to God, she was going to have to make silence a part of her day.

That is precisely what she has done. On her daily to-do list, she writes "Meditate in silence" and has made it a point to follow Mom's example and take twenty minutes or so for herself to sit in silence and let go of all the thoughts that pop into her mind. Some days, this can be harder to make time for than others, especially since her son came into her life. But what she has realized is that it is okay if her meditation does not look like sitting on a pillow with an erect back and fingers intertwined into a figure eight with Peruvian flute music playing softly in the background. Sometimes it's nursing her son in the rocking chair while he drifts off to sleep. She has found that as long as her eyes are closed and it's generally quiet, she is able to slow her thoughts, and she receives the benefits that she so loves from meditation.

Recently, Serena was chatting with her friend Shannon about the importance of having mantras and repeating them to yourself when you feel out of alignment. As they were talking, Shannon mentioned that she thought it was important to repeat these mantras while looking in the mirror, recognizing that we need to truly see and speak them to ourselves to feel the weight of each word. Suddenly, in the middle of the conversation, Serena felt as if Dad had spoken the words to a poem by Rumi he often recited when he was alive, one she had forgotten all about since his passing.

> You who seek God, apart, apart
> The thing you seek, thou art, thou art.
> If you wish to see the Beloved's face
> Polish the mirror, gaze into that space.[4]

As these words arose in her mind, she felt as though our dad was encouraging her to do exactly what she and Shannon had been discussing—to stop avoiding being herself and thinking that God and everything we desire is somehow separate from us. Instead, to remember, by gazing at our own reflection when repeating mantras, that God is within us, and if you are seeking God, go within, because that is where you will find God. This is a form of meditation onto itself, a means of obtaining conscious contact with God.

Author and publisher Louise Hay often taught that the most important and powerful affirmations are those that you say in front of the mirror, as the mirror reflects back to you the feelings you have about yourself. Mirror Work, as she called it, allows you to become immediately aware of what you are open to and what you are resisting. Meditation, or sitting in silence and allowing the gaps between your thoughts to expand, is one method of becoming more and more connected to your highest self, which is God. But mantras and affirmations, especially when done in front of the mirror, are another way of practicing the self-love that will guide you deeper and further in your own meditative practice.

Luckily for both of us, we have had exposure to many different forms of meditation, whether it was mantras, chants, silence, or affirmations. And of course, it doesn't hurt to have learned by example, as we both have from our parents' lifelong dedication to meditation.

THE QUIET DYER

When it comes to disciplined meditation and silence, our mom has been our best role model. For as long as we can remember, she has meditated every single day. As we've mentioned, she used to put that sign on her door: "Mom is meditating for TWENTY MINUTES . . . please do not disturb!" And trust us, even as small children, we honored it.

She has often told us, "I don't think we in this world honor silence enough. To me, it is my greatest tool." She asks anyone who is interested to consider meditating. Even if it's only for ten minutes, just sit in the same spot daily. She doesn't recommend a certain way—maybe it's listening to music or a guided meditation or watching a candle flame. She doesn't believe there is just one way to do anything, but as she has always said to us, when it comes to reaching peace and enlightenment, think about it like this: What if you live in Miami, but peace and enlightenment are located in Canada? How many ways are there to get there? By foot, plane, bus, car, back roads, highways . . . How many roadmaps? Enlightenment is personal, and the meditation you choose (and do!) is your way to reach it.

Another gift our mom gave us is an unorthodox but powerful form of meditation she calls her "love list." Here's how she describes it:

> With meditation comes an awareness of the essence of your thoughts, and that awareness is the key to me. Key to your happiness, to your peace, to your joy, to your acceptance, to your tolerance, to patience. If I could teach anything to anyone, it's that we all need to meditate. A lot of people will say, "I've tried it, and I can't get my mind to quiet." Don't worry about that. It takes time for the mind to be trained or ignored enough for you to realize that it isn't as loud as it was, because I believe the mind doesn't have the clarity that silence does. And that's where I believe with my teacher, Jesus. He went into the wilderness, the mountain for forty days and forty nights in silence. I mean, silence is vital to reaching a level of that kind of peace. It's a practice engaged by all the great spiritual teachers, and for each of them, silence is the key.

From a young age, I realized that my time on earth was limited. And because it's so limited, I wanted to get the most out of it. As a girl, I made it a point to attend every church in my town—Methodist, Lutheran, Presbyterian, Episcopalian, and Catholic. I talked to friends that were members and learned that there are beautiful tenets in every religion, but I still didn't have the answers. It seemed like the dogmas and the philosophies were more exclusive rather than inclusive. I didn't believe that one of the holiest people to walk this earth—Jesus—came here to teach us that we need to be separate instead of close to others and loving. So I forged my own path in search of truth and began to realize the limits of organized religion.

I was very fortunate to have parents who were quiet people, and hence my quietness. They felt no need to instill in me their religion or professions or even level of education. They trusted me to choose wisely and allowed me to seek my own answers. From the time I was twelve years old, I found that after prayer at night, I would close my ears with my thumbs to drown out the television downstairs and recite my "love list," naming every single person I had met.

I prayed for my parents, my grandparents, and my sister and brothers. Then I added my cousins and aunts and uncles. One of my cousins, Mikey, died as a young child in the church parking lot, as he was run over by a car. I prayed for him especially and his parents and siblings. I asked God to watch over my neighborhood and school and little town. The paper boy, because my older brother, Rich, delivered the morning local paper, and I saw how cold he was in the winter, and I prayed the other newspaper deliverers were safe and warm. I prayed for our church and the pastor and his family.

The store clerk at Penny Wise, because once I stole a bag of M&M's while there with my Mom, and he didn't scream at me but gave me his broom and asked me to sweep the entranceway, which I did. Afterward, he gave me a nickel, and he had my bag of M&M's in his hand. He told me now I could buy his bag of candy because I had earned a nickel, and that's what it cost. I was only four years old, but I listened to his explanation about how hard he worked to have this store and that everything has a price tag on it. He was kind and soft-spoken and taught me a great lesson. My mother stood aside and allowed him to teach me, which I always look back on with gratitude. I prayed for this store manager, that he would teach every thief in his kind way. My school and teachers were prayed for, that they were good to the students. I prayed that people in pain felt better. The hungry were given food. The thirsty were given water. And the homeless were given shelter. And then I prayed for everyone I knew and didn't know, that they were happy and healthy and loved.

At the end of my love list, I reached a place of serenity even though I wasn't aware of meditation at the time. I just thought that was part of prayer. It wasn't until I was forty-one and Wayne and I were introduced to the Transcendental Meditation technique that I realized I had been doing this all my life.

In our home, our mom never had the television on for background noise or the radio on in the car. It was always silent, and because there wasn't noise or talking heads to compete with, we all talked to each other. As a result, we have come to know that children feel seen when they are given the space to actually be heard. As a mother, Serena is often amazed at the times when she is in the car, driving her kids to and from school or activities, and turns the music off. Everyone starts talking and sharing jokes and stories from their days, eventually filling the car with laughter.

As we grew up, meditation was a sacred thing. Both our parents adopted a habit of meditating regularly, something that benefited our entire family and that we took for granted as children. We believe much of the peace, wisdom, and love that we grew up with was a direct result of their commitment to getting silent and practicing meditation. It made our home a peaceful one. There were never big fights or yelling or screaming. Of course there were conflicts, but they were always peaceful.

Dad was always a meditator, but we have to admit, his discipline was not as rigorous as Mom's. She truly never misses a day and has stuck to the same practice throughout her life. Dad was very interested in meditation and made it a regular practice, but he was always trying new methods and wasn't quite as strict and precise in his practice.

When Saje was in Australia with our dad during the weeks before he passed away, she, Skye, Mo, and our dad had adjoining rooms in almost every hotel they stayed in. Our dad would burst into our rooms each morning with his off-key rendition of "Oh what a beautiful morning—gosh what a beautiful day. I've got a wonderful feeling, everything's going my way!" Then, after pulling our covers off and opening the blinds to ensure that we were truly awake, he would declare that it was time to meditate! Ever since we were little kids, our dad would come into our room on Maui every summer morning, singing this same song!

During the Australia trip, he was really interested in a fifteen-minute practice repeating the phrase, "I am not the body; I am not even the mind" for about ten minutes, followed by breathing exercises and chanting the word *om*. So each morning, Skye and Saje were awakened to this beautiful phrase repeated, which soaked into their consciousness. To this day, the words still bring Saje comfort. She loves the idea that Dad was helping her to understand that when a few days later, as he left his body and his mind went with it, he had been neither of these things in the first place. That when Saje feels plagued by tiredness or negative thoughts, she is neither of these things anyway. And when her time comes to leave her body, she was never this to begin with, so she won't really be going anywhere. If Saje were to sum up the existential benefit that meditation has brought her as a whole, it is this: she is not her body and she is not her mind. Meditation gives her an awareness of the space between her body and her soul and between her mind and her soul.

Our parents created a home centered around peace, and as mothers, we've tried to emulate them. We've learned that sometimes what you are doing is so loud your kids can't hear what you're saying, so we do our best to model this Knowing for our children, reinforcing moments of stillness and listening to the universe.

MEDITATION BRINGS A MIRACLE

I close my eyes, and I feel peace. I can always choose peace, and peace is what I choose in this moment . . . Serena learned this meditation from our dad when they were on a trip in Europe and he was encouraging her to let go of a fight she had had with Matt. She practices it to this day to connect to her Knowing. As she puts it, "The more I get in that space, the more my subconscious marinates in it." When we were children, after going to other people's homes and often seeing how chaotic or loud or hectic they were, we both felt an awareness that our parents had fostered a home full of peace, and much of that came from their meditation practices. When Serena became a parent, she decided to embrace meditation with more intention than she had before, because she, too, wanted her home to be a serene home, and she wanted her children to experience what she had experienced with having two parents who were calm and joyful, especially after taking that twenty to thirty minutes each day to meditate.

As Carlos Castaneda wrote in his book, *Power of Silence*, "Silent knowledge is something that all of us have. . . . Something that has complete mastery, complete knowledge of everything. But it cannot think, therefore it cannot speak of what it knows. . . . Man gave up silent knowledge for the world of reason. . . . The more he clings to the world of reason, the more ephemeral *intent* becomes."[5] We all have our own Knowing. It lives within us and is available at all times. Invite silence into your life so that *it* can lead the way.

Serena first discovered this for herself in 2014 while on her honeymoon with Matt. She had been dreaming of getting pregnant and becoming a mother her entire life, and right after they were married, Serena knew she wanted to get pregnant immediately. The only problem was that she had gone months without having a normal menstrual cycle. As anyone who has ever wanted to get pregnant knows, you need to ovulate in order to get pregnant, and Serena had not ovulated for months.

When Serena and Matt landed on the island of Kauai, they were picked up in a taxi and driven to their hotel by a very friendly man who was native to Kauai and had lived there his entire life. His family on Kauai went back generations. Serena told him she had heard Hawaiian lore that Kauai was the birthplace of all of the islands. She had read about a magical waterfall called Honokohau Falls and wanted to visit it. The man explained that that particular waterfall would take weeks to reach, but Hanakapi'ai Falls was a direct tributary of that main one that could be reached through an eight-hour round-trip hike, but it was stunning and surely contained magical waters as well.

Serena and Matt decided to do the hike, and Serena was dumbfounded at just how difficult this trek actually was. She had never been super athletic and typically shied away from intense exercise. Finding herself hours into this hike with what felt like no end in sight left her feeling physically and emotionally exhausted, especially after having to walk on extremely narrow paths some eight hundred feet up in the air and climb across raging rivers and jagged rocks. After many hours, Serena and Matt finally reached the falls and were overcome by the beauty of the water cascading down the mountain, dropping two hundred feet into a sunlit pool surrounded by trees and hanging moss.

Serena told Matt she needed to meditate, then she sat on a rock in the pool, closed her eyes, and began thanking God for getting her there in one piece and for the opportunity to see such a beautiful sight. Then she asked God to help her become pregnant with a healthy baby. She casually mentioned it being a girl, being kind, intelligent, creative, beautiful, and full of compassion. After saying her prayer, she continued to meditate. After she and Matt swam in the water for a bit, they made the long hike back and eventually reached the home of friends who lived nearby, Roberta and Gordon Haas.

Roberta and Gordon are a lovely couple who have lived on Kauai for decades and built a cathedral of a house surrounded by all the natural beauty of Kauai. At one point, when they were all conversing, Gordon looked at Serena and randomly said, "Do you hope to get pregnant?" Serena replied that she did, and he asked her if she were to get pregnant that very day, and it was a girl, what would she name her? Serena said that she hadn't really discussed the name with Matt, but ever since she was a little girl, she had wanted to have a daughter named Sailor. Gordon then got up and returned with a box of three children's books that he had written in the 1970s, the Courtney Flower series. He took out the first book and signed it "To Sailor, love Gordon, 7/19/14." After a wonderful visit, Serena and Matt, with Gordon's books in hand, returned to their hotel to enjoy the rest of their honeymoon.

A few weeks after returning home, Serena felt sick and nauseous over every little thing. She still had not had a regular cycle, so she did not imagine she could be pregnant until one of her friends basically demanded she take a pregnancy test. She did, and it was positive!

When Serena called her obstetrician to schedule her first appointment, they asked her the first date of her last period to determine how far along she was, and she told them she hadn't had a period in months, so they scheduled for her to come in that same week. At the first ultrasound exam, Serena's doctor showed them the beating heart and took a bunch of measurements to determine the actual date of conception. The doctor explained that the very first measurements are incredibly accurate in giving a due date, and after taking the measurements and putting them in the computer, the doctor told Serena and Matt that they must have conceived on July 19, 2014. When Serena got home, she immediately opened those children's books because she had a sudden Knowing that the date her baby was conceived was the exact date Gordon had signed the books to her future daughter.

In October, when Serena did a test to determine the sex of the baby, she was anxiously waiting to find out if she was indeed having a girl when she received a text from the friend who had introduced her to Roberta and Gordon. It said that Gordon had passed away that morning. No more than an hour later, her doctor called her to tell her that she was in fact pregnant with a little girl!

Although these remarkable events did lead to the conception and birth of Sailor, it goes without saying that anyone who has had or is having fertility issues might scoff at the idea that simply meditating on getting pregnant creates the space for one to conceive. For Serena, though, it feels apparent that Sailor was predestined to arrive at the time she did, but perhaps Serena had to simply get out of her own way and surrender through meditation.

Serena believes that when Gordon was returning to the place from which we all originate, he gave a little wave to her daughter Sailor as she was heading in the opposite direction on this earthly circuit we all experience. After finding out Sailor was a girl and that Gordon had passed, she decided to sit down and read his children's book to the baby that was growing inside her. When she got to the page that said "Meditation brings a miracle," she let out a stifled sob, knowing full well the power in those words. Meditation surely does bring a miracle.

A Way of Knowing

How can I still my mind and hear my heart?

Many people use prayer as a form of meditation, and often we will begin a meditation with a prayer of gratitude, but as our father always said, if prayer is you talking to God, meditation is God talking to *you*. When we allow the space within ourselves that is connected to God or the universe or consciousness, we allow the guidance we are seeking to enter. If our minds are filled with noise, we never have the chance to hear what greater Knowing we are being given.

Meditation, for Serena and Saje, does not look like burning incense, chanting, sitting cross-legged on the floor, and repeating mantras. If it looks like that for someone else, more power to them! Meditation does not have a time limit. It does not have a dress code or a set of rules. All meditation asks of us is that we show up for it. Whatever form it takes for you is perfectly acceptable, and it seems plausible that everyone's meditation practice is unique to them. For Serena, meditation means closing her eyes, observing the thoughts that continually try to cross her mind, and breathing deeply until the thoughts abate and ultimately are not there at all. It is incredible that when one goes into a meditation with a certain fear or situation they need guidance on, after sitting in silence for twenty minutes or so, one can emerge with the Knowing to clarify that burning question or situation or provide the salve to the wound that fear creates.

We believe that the universe offers its guidance by speaking to us as our thoughts. We know this may sound a little funny or odd. But have you ever had profound thoughts pop into your head seemingly out of nowhere? Or a flash of insight? Or have you ever had a thought in which you addressed yourself in a way that would be unusual? For instance, a thought that starts with "My love" or "Sweetheart." We don't know about you, but we don't usually address ourselves this way, and we believe this is the universe or even our spirit guides or passed-on loved ones speaking directly to us through our universal mind. Our friend Karen Noe advised us to watch out for thoughts that start this way, and since bringing some awareness to this, we've both noticed the difference. The key, though, is creating silence in your own mind in order to hear the guidance you are seeking. If we never turn off the noise in our head, how will we experience how, as Herman Melville wrote, "Silence is the only Voice of our God"?[6]

Recently, Saje was shopping in a department store, and out of nowhere, she started to recite lines from that Elizabeth Barret Browning poem our dad loved so much:

Earth's crammed with heaven,
And every common bush afire with God;
But only he who sees, takes off his shoes,
The rest sit round it and pluck blackberries . . . [7]

Saje had heard Dad recite these lines many times before, but they weren't active in her consciousness, nor could she remember the last time she had even thought about this poem. She recognized in that moment that perhaps this was the universe communicating with her. Then when she went to check out, her total came to $77.77, which was the confirmation she needed that she was experiencing some guidance or some divine alignment. When she got home, she looked up the meaning of repeating sevens on Google and found many references saying that repeating number sevens indicate "intuition, mysticism, inner wisdom, and a deep inward *knowing*." (Which we just happened to put in Chapter 7!)

Guidance like this is always being offered to us, but if our minds are crammed with thoughts, to-do lists, and judgments, we will not be able to tune in. Meditation is essentially a practice of quieting the mind, and the mind is a muscle; the more you quiet it, the easier it becomes to quiet it, and the quieter it gets. When the mind is quiet, deep inner Knowings make themselves heard. We are more in tune with our intuition and with the universal mind that is always available to all of us.

When we embrace meditation or silence, we give our bodies the chance to adapt to the world of noise and triggers that we all encounter on a daily basis. When we are able to meet chaos with a peaceful mind, we become healthier, happier, and more able to deal with our perceived problems. We become less likely to react from a place that we might regret later, especially when we encounter those times in life at which we need to forgive someone or even ourselves.

When you sit down to meditate, we suggest you start out with an intention. Saje likes to state to herself, "Dear Universe, please allow these next twenty minutes to serve to clear my mind and tune me in to the universal guidance that is always available to me." Some people prefer to use a guided meditation, but what we have learned from our mom, who we consider the master meditator, is that silence is the best practice. After all, the goal of meditation is to create silence in your mind or to tune into the space between your thoughts. As you meditate, thoughts will continue to arise, and that is perfectly normal. The best way to get yourself back to the silence is to simply forgive the thoughts and tune back in. This will likely happen again and again, and all you have to do each time you notice that you have drifted once more is to bring yourself back to your intention of tuning into the universal guidance that comes in the form of silence.

Instead of offering a guided meditation, we would like to offer a short visualization that has helped us to stay on track during our meditation practice. Picture yourself as a passenger on a slow-moving train, with the train being the vessel that moves you deeper into the silence. Your thoughts will attempt to jump onto your train. However, you continuously just move steadily along, and these thoughts are left to fade away in the distance. Thoughts can be anything from going over all the things you need to do that day to revisiting a distant memory to ruminating on the things that make you fearful. The content does not matter. All you need to do is continually remember not to indulge in them as you move forward on your train. Allow this visualization to guide your mind to a place of stillness until you no longer need it, and then let it go as you settle into meditative bliss. We recommend carving out twenty minutes every single day for meditation. If you are able to stick to this for just a couple of weeks, you will notice that you begin to crave your meditation in the same way that you crave food or sleep. Even more importantly, you will notice how your entire way of being shifts into one of greater alignment and peace.

CHAPTER 8

The Geometry of Forgiveness

"When we love ourselves, we refuse to allow
others to manage our emotions from afar.
Forgiveness is our means to that end."

DR. WAYNE W. DYER,
EVERYDAY WISDOM

MASON

Forgiveness is not only a tool we need to offer to someone who has wronged us. Forgiveness is also incredibly important when we offer it to ourselves. Loving someone who supports you, who provides for you, who adores you—like we loved our dad—is not a difficult task. Loving someone who challenges you, who forces you to grow, is much more difficult.

In February of 2009, Serena first met Matt at a dinner party in Miami. They fell in love. Shortly after that first encounter, Serena met Matt's ten-year-old son, Mason, who was a quiet and shy little boy, devoted to his father, and open to getting to know her. Her relationship with Mason paralleled that with Matt, since he pretty much lived with his father full time. Serena moved in with Matt about a year after they met, and still in her early twenties, she became a stepparent to Mason, even though there was only a thirteen-year age difference. Because of her immaturity at times or her insecurity about Matt and Mason's close relationship, she clashed with Mason, especially in the early years.

Looking back, she recognizes that at first, she viewed Mason as a competitor for Matt's affection. She basically wanted Matt to herself—she didn't want to share a hotel room with Mason when they took vacations together, and she wanted to build her relationship with Matt without having a child to contend with. This led to many fights between Serena and Matt, as he was unwilling to make his son secondary to her. It grew clear his son was his priority, and he was not willing to make him less of one for her (in hindsight) childish whims.

She can look back over the years of living with Matt and Mason and feel incredible guilt over how often she wanted to cast Mason aside, how often she wanted him to go to a friend's house or have a sleepover somewhere else so she and Matt could be alone. She found a thousand small things to be upset or offended over. She would freak out over dishes left in the sink or his smelly lacrosse shoes on the stairs. She initiated fights with Matt, Mason, or both of them over things she now sees were nonevents.

Serena can also reflect on the many wonderful things that she did with and for Mason, like insisting on family dinner with the three of them every night and excitedly discussing world events with him. She became really involved in helping him with his schoolwork—quizzing him on vocabulary words before a test and celebrating his good grades. She threw birthday parties for him and, as he got older, loved helping him pick out a Valentine's gift for his girlfriend or taking him shopping for a new outfit for a school dance. As the years progressed, her relationship with Mason grew in a meaningful way. After Matt proposed to her in 2012 and they were engaged, she no longer felt threatened by the bond between father and son and instead began to view Mason as her own family. The three of them grew even closer after Matt and Serena were married, and Mason gave an incredible speech at their wedding, thanking both Matt and Serena for believing in him.

Even though Serena had been hard on him at times, the love she felt for Mason continued to grow and blossomed when Sailor was born. He was a wonderful big brother, and the love he felt for his little sister was palpable. There might have still been times when she became frustrated with him, but he was a teenager, after all, and forgot his chores and left messes around the house. But as they both grew up, they developed a deep mutual respect.

Around the time Mason was seventeen years old, he started to experiment with drugs. Matt and Serena were both aware that he had been smoking pot and occasionally drinking at parties with his friends, but they took a sort of hands-off approach to this, assuming it was normal teenage behavior and would sort itself out as he got older. As long as he continued to work his job as a busser, do well in school, and play sports, they decided not to make a big deal about it. When Serena and Matt were high school students, they both drank at parties or tried smoking pot with their friends, so in some ways, they felt hypocritical for punishing him for these things.

It was a dark time. Matt's court case was looming. Mason's drug use escalated, and Matt and Serena discovered he was experimenting with pills. They began to fight with him about this, resulting in Mason being grounded, losing his phone or computer privileges. They thought these consequences were working until Mason left Xanax pills out where toddler Sailor could reach them, almost set the kitchen on fire, and started getting bad grades. The consequence was a particularly long period of being grounded in which Mason could only go to and from school and was regularly drug tested. He stayed clean and started to do well in his classes again, so Matt and Serena thought they had a handle on things and Mason could go back to hanging out with his friends. Within one week, his school called, asking them to pick him up because he was intoxicated.

Mason was eighteen years old, a senior in high school at the time, and Matt was at a breaking point. Mason and Matt had a huge fight that basically resulted in Matt kicking his son out of the house. Serena remembers listening to the argument, occasionally jumping in herself, and feeling like she had completely failed at being a stepmother. Our parents had never correlated our self-worth with our grades, athletic ability, or accomplishments, and yet she and Matt had made those things key points of focus. In the first two years of her relationship with Matt, Serena wished Mason would live with someone else so she and Matt could be alone. Now Matt was essentially telling him to get out, and Serena felt enormously guilty, as if she had somehow caused this. After the argument,

Mason had his girlfriend pick him up, and he ended up going to his friend's house for the night.

The following day, Serena called Mason and asked him to meet her at a park so she could talk to him and ask him to make amends with Matt so that he could come home. She poured her heart out to Mason at that park and told him that for years, she had not wanted him there, but now, more than anything, she wanted him to come home. She wanted him to apologize to his dad for bringing drugs into the home, she wanted a second chance at parenting him from a place of love and total acceptance, and she wanted him to feel that they were a family and could get through this together. She told him that she loved him, that she wanted them to be a family, and that his dad did as well.

Later that day, Mason came home. He and Matt had a beautiful conversation, and Serena felt even more committed to making Mason feel loved.

Things went well at first, but after a few weeks, Mason realized that unless he got out of south Florida, away from the temptations of peers and pills, he would not make it. Matt and Serena were proud of him for realizing he needed to get out of this situation, and they agreed to let him go live with a friend in Georgia, away from these temptations. He stayed in Georgia for about a week but ended up falling in with some kids who used drugs. After getting kicked out of the friend's house in Georgia, he went to live on an Army base in Texas with his aunt, uncle, and their teenage children, whom Mason had hung out with a lot when he was younger. He was excited to go stay with them and give his sobriety a second chance.

HOʻOPONOPONO

Soon after the birth of Serena's second daughter, Windsor, we all celebrated the one-year anniversary of our dad's death at our mom's house with most of the family. Skye sang the Prayer of Saint Francis:

> . . . grant that I may
> Not so much seek to be consoled as to console
> To be understood, as to understand
> To be loved, as to love
> For it is in giving that we receive
> And it's in pardoning that we are pardoned . . . [1]

Serena immediately started crying, moved by Skye's beautiful voice and thinking back to how many times she had heard her sister sing that very song while on stage with our dad at one of his lectures. As she headed home, she had a weird feeling, as if she were driving in the car with our dad. She felt incredibly light, weightless, and stress free, and she could smell our dad. It was the nicest feeling in the world.

She told Matt about it, and as they talked, she realized that in that moment, Dad was trying to help her remember peace, that it exists inside her and is always available. He was saying that she did not have to wait for the stress of the legal troubles and Mason's difficulties and being a mom to go away to feel peace. In fact, she had to bring that feeling of peace back to herself. She had to remember what peace felt like, and if she did so, the stress would go away on its own.

Serena realized she had been doing it wrong all along. She had been waiting for the pieces of her life to fall into place so that she could then be peaceful, even though she had been raised on the idea that she must first become peaceful *within* herself in order for the pieces to fall into place. She had been dreaming about all of the issues and problems of her life going away and was picturing herself living on Maui with her family, believing that once that happened, she would finally have internal peace. Maui was her version of paradise, her own Tahiti, and she was so obsessed with dreaming about living there once the legal drama was over that she completely forgot what Herman Melville actually meant when he wrote, "So in the soul of man lies one insular Tahiti." She suddenly became acutely aware that she had abandoned her own insular Tahiti and convinced herself that the only way she could achieve real peace was by living on Maui, free from the troubles she had been experiencing. In having this moment of clarity, she realized that within herself, she could find Maui, or the "insular Tahiti" Melville was describing, and that *becoming like what it was she was seeking* was the only way to actually get in alignment with her desires.

As Dad often said, "Serena, we don't get what we want, we get what we *are*, so *become* what it is you desire, and the universe will bring what you desire into your life." Serena had been raised on this idea, that everything is energy, and for every action or thought, there is an equal and opposite reaction. It is the law of attraction. And she realized that she had been living from a place of fear and lack, and therefore, she continued to receive more of the experiences that were in alignment with the energy and thoughts she was giving out to the universe. She could actually hear our dad's voice say, "Just remember, Serena, what people do is their karma, but how you react is yours. You can always choose peace rather than this."

Serena realized that she could not end by staying in the same energy field that had created her feelings in the first place. To have the situation change, she had to start by changing herself. She logically understood this from our dad's teachings but had never really applied it to her life. The experience with him in the car reminded her that she had, within herself, everything she needed to create the life she wanted for herself, Matt, Mason, Sailor, and Windsor. She was reminded that although she couldn't always choose the circumstances of her life, she could choose how she viewed those circumstances, and that would make all the difference in the world. She began exerting a conscious effort to tap into the power of intention, to go within, to find peace rather than looking outside of herself and expecting everything else to change.

As she began the practice of bringing peace into her home by meditating and writing, she was stunned to watch the transformation Matt was simultaneously experiencing. He began the practice of Ho'oponopono, which is the ancient Hawaiian practice of reconciliation and forgiveness based on this prayer:

> I am sorry.
> Please forgive me.
> Thank you.
> I love you.

As he prepared for the trial of his life, the trial in which his very freedom was on the line, he changed before her eyes from a man who was driven to achieve financial success with very little concern for risk to a man whose sole purpose became forgiving not only himself but anyone who was part of the prosecution and the business that he had not believed was ever illegal.

Not only did he work on forgiveness, he began to send love, light, and healing to every member of the prosecution team. He became a different person, much more patient with strangers, more loving and expressive toward his family and friends, and increasingly focused not on financial success but on personal growth. It reminded Serena of the "morning and afternoon of your life" from the writings of Carl Jung that our dad so often spoke about. Jung described the morning of your life as the time occupied by ambition, acquiring accolades and wealth, impressing people, and fulfilling the needs of the ego, which tell us that who we are is what we have or what people think of us or what we do for a living. The afternoon of your life, which can begin at any age, depending on the individual, is when we shift our focus from ambition to meaning. The afternoon of your life represents the time when you move away from ego and toward finding meaning in your time on earth. If the morning of your life is based on achieving success, the afternoon of your life becomes about honoring whatever it is you feel called to do in your soul.

Matt seemed to be entering the afternoon of his life, and even though this shift was brought about by outside forces—the prosecutors who were wanting to send him to prison and the challenges with Mason—it was the way he responded to this crisis that led Serena to know he was moving away from ambition, away from fighting the prosecution and "winning," instead concentrating his energy on love, on forgiveness, on understanding.

These truths would help Matt and Serena endure the dark times ahead.

A NEW TEACHER EMERGES

Everything had been going well for Mason in Texas, and eventually, he convinced Matt and Serena to send him a ticket so that he could fly back to Florida to go to the prom with his high school friends. Mason was back for about a week, and although it was fun to have him with them, and they were all happy to be together, it was clear he was back to partying hard with his friends. Matt's trial was coming up, and the stress of that was enough to cause Matt and Serena to decide that it was best for her to take Sailor and their new baby, Windsor, to Maui for a while and keep them away from the anxious energy the trial was creating. Mason volunteered to help Serena travel with the babies to Maui, and so the four of them went together, Mason helping her throughout the course of the twelve-hour flight. When they arrived in Maui, Mason said he wanted to return to Texas, so Matt and Serena bought him a ticket. Serena gave him a hug while standing in the kitchen of our dad's condo as he got ready to leave in a cab. She told him she loved him and said goodbye.

After Texas, Mason made his way to North Carolina, where his mom lived. He met a girl there, and one day in

September 2017, soon after the two-year anniversary of our dad's passing, Mason called Serena, excited to tell her he was in love for the first time and how much it meant that she, his mom, and his dad were all supporting him. Mason had not had a consistent relationship with his mom, and he was happy to be reconnected with her. Mason's mother and Serena began communicating more frequently about Mason, and he was aware that everyone was looking out for him, which helped him feel loved. During the phone call, he told Serena that he loved her, that he was going to make her proud. She promised him that she loved him and was already proud of him.

Four days later, Serena was at home with both of her daughters when Matt called. She knew he was supposed to be in a lawyers' meeting, so she was surprised to see his name pop up on her phone. He couldn't speak; his voice was quaking.

"What's wrong?" she asked. Matt wasn't forming actual words. His voice was strange and choked as he let out a sound she will never forget. Then Matt said the words that would forever haunt them.

"Mason died."

Serena felt as if the strength in her legs had gone and she was going to fall over, almost like she was out of her body. All she could say was "Oh my God . . . oh my God." Matt told her he had left his meeting, didn't even know where he was, and was walking along the road, unable to process this. Serena immediately called Skye to come watch the girls so she could go find her grief-stricken husband.

When she did, he was at the beach, sitting in the sand with his head in his hands, sobbing and repeating one word again and again: *Why?* Serena asked Matt if Mason's mom knew, and he said that he didn't think she knew, because the detective had called Matt even though Mason was in North Carolina, where his mom lived. Serena's hands were uncontrollably shaking as she placed the call to Mason's mother and had to deliver the news that he had passed, because his mother did not in fact know. The purest form of grief and sadness, tenderness and love overtook her as she delivered the news to Mason's mother, the woman who had brought him into this world, knowing that the death of her precious son would forever change her life as well.

What happened next was a blur of phone calls, guests arriving from out of town, funeral arrangements, and planning and organizing the service to honor Mason's life. Serena wanted to hold her husband, to carry the weight of what he was feeling, and relieve him of his suffering, all the while processing her own grief, loss, sense of failure, and, most significantly, guilt. She felt that she had caused this. Inwardly, she felt deep, deep regret—if only she had loved Mason more, had expressed her own insecurities sooner, perhaps he would never have turned to drugs.

After our father died, Serena longed for him because the love they shared was great and was a source of pure inspiration in her life. After Mason died, she felt a totally different type of grief. She felt she wasn't even worthy of grieving for him because she felt responsible for his death. In the days and weeks after Mason passed away, Matt would regularly wear Mason's clothes, his smelly lacrosse jersey, his favorite sweater, and when she would hug Matt, she would smell Mason.

She couldn't understand why she had spent so many years being upset that Mason wore his sweaty jersey on the couch or at the dinner table and why she had made that a focus instead of loving him. She would have given anything to be able to go back and see him wearing his jersey on the couch, his dirty dishes in the sink, or his shoes on the stairs. She'd wasted too much time focusing on mundane, meaningless things rather than loving him and making sure he felt her love. The guilt she felt in the weeks and months after Mason passed away was enough to make her hate herself for allowing human errors to get in the way of our soul's purpose, which is simply to love and be loved in return. She no longer felt worthy of love and was ashamed at the very core of her being. She knew that there had been a ton of goodness shared between her and Mason, but none of that compared to the shame she felt.

Matt tried to talk her out of it, pointing out all of the fun and joyful times she'd been a part of in Mason's life, and he encouraged her to think of Mason in the space of joy, of love, as she had done after her father's death, so that Mason could perhaps come to her and help her process his death. Her beloved husband was experiencing the greatest loss imaginable, and yet he was trying to comfort Serena. For Matt's sake, she promised to contemplate the love Mason and she had shared, but inwardly, she was committed to her shame.

Then, one evening as she drifted off to sleep, Serena had a sudden memory of laughing with Mason over how scared they both were after watching a horror movie. She felt a little bit of peace and started to fall asleep. This was the first time since Mason had passed away that she did not toss and turn in anxiety over her guilt. That night, Mason appeared to her in a dream that felt real. He was standing in the hallway of their home, holding Sailor, and they were dancing to music. She saw him, and he was glowing, his skin was golden, and he was emanating a type of love so pure that she felt overjoyed by his presence.

In the dream, she asked him if she could touch him. He held his hands out to her, and he was smiling so brightly that it was as if the whole room was glowing in a gold light. She asked him how he was, and he said, "Great!" She asked him if he knew she loved him, and he said, "Yes." Then she asked if he loved her, and he laughed, acting as though she were ridiculous, before once again replying, "Yes." She then asked him to forgive her, and he laughed again and said, "Yes." Serena felt overwhelming relief and apologized for ever causing him any pain. She asked him if he had seen our dad, and he said that he had! He had a twinkle in his eye that made Serena feel that they had been joking about something. Mason then got very serious and said that before he left, he had to tell her something. He said, "Serena, new teachers are emerging. You need to know that."

She felt him slipping away and woke up with tears of joy and love falling from her eyes. She shook Matt awake and told him Mason had been there with her, that he was happy and glowing, and Matt started crying as well.

Mason had given her a gift, and as she contemplated it, his role in her life transformed. She was able to look at everything in a different light, considering that per-haps they had come into each other's lives exactly as they needed to, for he had come to teach her and all who knew him about forgiveness, particularly forgiveness for ourselves. She began to look back and feel incredible gratitude for getting to know him, to love him, to be his stepmother. She felt grateful for his life-altering teaching: living a life from a place that is anything other than love was not a worthwhile life to live. Nothing mattered in life but loving someone and knowing that they feel your love, and she came to realize that Mason had indeed felt her love, that she hadn't failed.

Mason continues to appear in her dreams from time to time, always glowing, always offering unconditional love and forgiveness. It is because of the love he has given her that she has been able to forgive herself. Our dad loved this quote by an unknown author: "Forgiveness is the fragrance that the violet sheds on the heel that has crushed it." There is no more fitting line to express the type of grace she feels has come from her relationship with her friend, son, and teacher Mason.

A Way of Knowing

A simple prayer can change your life
and the lives of those around you.

Our parents' mutual forgiveness after they chose not to divorce led to a different and somehow closer family. For Serena, when she talks about Mason with her children or spends time in his room or makes a cake with her daughters to celebrate Mason's birthday, she does this from a place of joy. The connection she feels to Mason is stronger now than ever before, and she knows he is constantly surrounding all of them with love, the same love she sends back to him. Mason, more than anyone else, taught Serena about the power of forgiveness, and once she was able to forgive herself for any of the negativity she brought into her relationship with him while he was alive, she was able to connect with him from a place of only love. When she does, she often relies on the Ho'oponopono prayer.

Ho'oponopono is a Hawaiian prayer wherein you simply repeat four lines, over and over again, while thinking of who you would like to forgive or receive forgiveness from:

> I am sorry.
> Please forgive me.
> Thank you.
> I love you.

When saying "I am sorry," it doesn't always mean that you were wrong. It can be an acknowledgment of your soul's need to have the other person appear in your life for whatever they were here to teach you and also to acknowledge whatever harm you may have done to them.

"Please forgive me" is based on the idea that we called this person into our life for a reason, and whatever that reason might be, we may ask to be forgiven for needing this exchange to further our soul's growth in the first place.

"Thank you" is about honoring whoever this person is and your gratitude for the role they played in your life, even if it was a negative one like our dad experienced with his own father before forgiving him at his father's grave. Thanking the person for being in your life, no matter what form they took, is about honoring the role they played, good or bad. As our dear friend, the spiritual teacher Baba Ram Dass, famously said, "We are all just walking each other home." Wherever we might be on our individual paths toward enlightenment or Christ-consciousness or radical self-acceptance, we can thank everyone and everything for showing up in our lives when they did. Their role, good or bad, helped us get closer to where we want to be, but only when we choose to see it as all divinely orchestrated to begin with.

"I love you" is self-explanatory. That which is not love is fear, and that which is not fear is love. Love is what is everlasting, the force that unites us all.

When we repeat this Ho'oponopono prayer, we become closer to God, for God does not blame, condemn, or find fault. God is always providing, always loving, always accepting of what is, not what we think it ought to be. Looking at your life, how many times did you have a chance to forgive someone who hurt you—even if that person was yourself—but instead remained steadfast in your commitment to punish or hurt that person in return? How many times a day do we encounter a time when we can prove that we were "right" or "justified" in our anger or resentment—and how often does that commitment to your own lower emotions prevent you from receiving the miracle you have been seeking all along?

CHAPTER 9

Yielding to the Signs

"The hard and stiff will be broken . . . the soft
and supple will prevail. When we see ourselves
as flexible and supple, we can bend in harmony
with our Divine source. By listening, yielding, and
being gentle, we all become disciples of life."

DR. WAYNE W. DYER,
"STAY LOOSE"

LET THERE BE LIGHT

Our dad sometimes called coincidences "winks from God,"
but it isn't until we let go of our attachment to how these
coincidences occur or our need to control the outcome
that we can see them. Near the end of 2017, Matt and
Serena were dealing not only with the loss of Mason but
with Matt's upcoming sentencing after being convicted
on one count of mail fraud during his trial earlier that
year. Serena found herself looking forward to the day of
sentencing so they could, in a way, get on with their lives.
She believed that once we knew what the sentence would
be, Matt would then begin serving his time, and each day

would be one day closer to waking up from the entire legal nightmare. She longed for a future in which all of this was over, which was ironic, as she had spent the last few years leading up to this longing for the past.

Then the other shoe dropped. In November, Matt was sentenced to seven years in prison. It sounded like an eternity. Their toddler, Sailor, would be nine and baby Windsor would be eight when he was released. She was terrified that her daughters' hearts would break when they realized that their daddy wasn't coming home anytime soon. The gift of Matt's legal situation was that it had forced him to stop working when Sailor was only two months old, so her entire life she had known Matt and Serena as full-time parents. The father he had become was beautiful to witness; he was extremely involved in everything from diaper changes to playdates, putting them to bed, making meals, and everything in between. The idea of him suddenly being out of their lives except for weekend visits to a federal prison camp was beyond Serena's comprehension.

Although Serena knew she would miss her husband, someone to share love and laughter and family with, it was the idea that his children would not have him around that truly broke her heart. Somehow, they continued to get out of bed each morning, celebrate the holidays with each other, and appreciate the time they had before his surrender date. All the while, they tried to maintain some sense of normalcy for their daughters, who not only had just lost their brother but were unaware they were about to say goodbye to their daddy for a long time as well.

On the morning Serena and Matt were set to leave for Pensacola for Matt to begin his sentence at the federal prison there, they said goodbye to the girls. Serena had planned to take Matt up to Pensacola herself. It all felt surreal. She watched as he hugged his daughters and told them he would be back, both blissfully unaware of what was really set to happen.

Serena and Matt flew to New Orleans and rented a car to drive to Pensacola. As they were setting the GPS, Matt's attorney called and said that they should stay in New Orleans for the time being. The prosecution that had tried Matt's case had filed a motion that essentially indicated they had withheld evidence and lied during the trial. Serena and Matt were stunned—completely in shock. They didn't know what to do with themselves, as it seemed too good to be true, and they couldn't understand why the prosecution would essentially tattle on themselves on the eve of his surrender.

They drove in circles, totally lost. They had no idea whether they should stay in New Orleans, make the drive to Pensacola, or fly back to Fort Lauderdale. They kept getting disoriented while driving aimlessly, so they decided to park the rental car in the parking lot of the Harrah's casino in downtown New Orleans and go for a walk. The very moment they pulled into the Harrah's parking area, a car zoomed up behind them. Serena turned to look, because she thought the car was going to plow into them in its haste. The car stopped right behind theirs, and she was shocked to see that the front license plate on the vehicle said "DANGER." The frame surrounding the plate said "Mason" on the top and "Let there be light" on the bottom. She excitedly exclaimed, "Matt, look!" and as he did, his cell phone started to ring. It was his attorney.

Serena watched the range of emotions on Matt's face as he listened to the call, eventually becoming covered head to toe in goose bumps and slowly going down on his knees. After he hung up, she couldn't believe it when he said, "The judge stayed the prison surrender. We aren't going in."

At the eleventh hour, the miracle they had prayed for had happened. She started laughing and crying and sneezing and snotting all at once. She called our family and told them that she and Matt would be on the first flight home in the morning, that Matt wasn't going to prison, that some miracle had occurred, because the prosecution was finally admitting how corrupt they had been during the trial and the events leading up to it.

Serena believes in her heart that, somehow, Mason had a hand in all of this. It was too much of a coincidence that in the moment they got the call from Matt's attorney, a license plate that indicated "danger" and was surrounded by "Mason" and "Let there be light" appeared right behind them.

NEXT PHASE DR. M. UNSTOPPABLE

After Dad's death, Serena continued to look for a deeper understanding. Throughout the journey she had been on during the last few difficult years, she had become aware of those peculiar moments that occurred in which she had suddenly felt an urgent call to look at something or pay attention to something and sit down to write. That was the kind of moment our dad would describe as being *unstoppable*, a force so strong that you no longer have a hold on it, but it has a hold on you, and it will take you to where you need to go.

One night, she got into bed with her children and started reading the latest novel she'd picked up. She was enjoying the book but kept feeling a quiet but urgent call to go back and read through the emails our dad had sent her while he was alive. She had done this before, and although some of the emails had been touching, like him asking for updated videos and photos of Sailor or sending random dad jokes, none had been powerful enough to force her out of a warm bed next to her two sleeping girls and husband.

She got out of bed and scrolled through the emails he had sent her over the years. One thread caught her eye, mostly because it was a conversation between Dad and Dr. Maithri Goonetilleke, a man he had met through a series of interesting connections and synchronicities. Dr. Goonetilleke is a doctor, public health advocate, and professor of epidemiology and preventive medicine based in Sydney, Australia. In 2013, when Dad was heading there to give a series of lectures, he was in a lot of pain, suffering from a trapped nerve in his neck, and he was concerned about whether he could actually get up in front of a live audience of thousands of people several days in a row and complete his lectures.

In the last three years of our dad's life, he experienced gripping nerve pain in his neck that was so debilitating he began wondering if his writing career was over, because the tilting of his head when he picked up the pen was enough to make his knees buckle in agony. It was essentially a bulging disc and pinched nerve, and despite the natural remedies he tried, he soon wondered if invasive neck surgery would be his only option. As the weeks and months went on, the neck pain persisted, but still he continued writing, saying he felt a sense of urgency that he had to finish *I Can See Clearly Now*. He also continued to study ancient texts, including Baird T. Spalding's *Life and Teaching of the Masters of the Far East*, *I AM Discourses of Saint Germain*, Paul F. Gorman's *The Impersonal Self*, and Swami Venkatesananda's *Vasistha's Yoga*, all about one specific topic: divine love.

In typical Dad fashion, he still got on the flight to Australia and was set on performing at the level he knew was expected of him, because people were counting on him. When he landed in Australia, he met with Dr. Goonetilleke, and they spent some time together assessing his neck, but beyond that, they had a deep conversation about love in general. After that meeting, as our dad lay in his hotel room, preparing for the next day's talk, he sent an email to his new friend, Maithri Goonetilleke, and for some reason, he cc'd Serena.

> My dearest Maithri . . . your beautiful words penetrate my heart and give me strength as I prepare to meditate on tomorrow's presentation. Our meeting was indeed Kismet personified. Our times together have illuminated a new light path for me in my time ahead. This pain from a trapped nerve in my neck is a reminder to me to think of all those children you serve so magnanimously as well as those imprisoned lost souls whose suffering is lessened by your commitment to be an instrument of service to ALL of humanity.
>
> And to put love where some kind of unconscious fear resides. I will be fine tomorrow. In precisely 12

hours I will be honored and humbled to speak of divine love, and meeting your joyful family was an example for me of seeing it all played out in perfect timing.

I know our meeting was miraculous for you, but it was equally enriching for me in a multitude of ways. I so appreciate your willingness to be here with me in person as my stellar physician and newfound spiritual brother, but your presence is felt not only now as I prepare to meditate, but it will accompany me throughout my time on stage in the morning. I have been sent a completely new message to deliver, and a way of making it a divine conversation rather than a performance for entertaining and educating the audience. It will be softer, gentler, and delivered through the meaning of the Hafiz poem "In a Treehouse" which speaks of the god-realization that represents mankind's ultimate destiny while here . . . indeed Earth is crammed with heaven, and I intend to get that message across in spades, in a fashion never before delivered by me. In no small way is that due to our serendipitous meetings in Melbourne at the venue, the hospital, my hotel, and your sweet sweet home filled with angels of kindness and mercy.

I am entering a new phase in my life. That ladder that Rumi spoke of which was placed before us at our birth to assist us in escaping from this world has each rung sequenced to move us to the place where we know that bliss is our TRUE STATE and this comes from finally living from a god realized place all the time. That's where the ladder's rungs come to a stop and there are no more objects comprised of particles. It's pure energy manifested as love.

I do not suffer my friend, I simply ask, how may I serve and encourage others to make the kinds of choices that we both spoke of so passionately. If it takes a pain in the neck to kick me in the ass and deliver from an even more compassionate place, then hallelujah I rejoice in it.

I treasure our connection Maithri, it was ordained long before you read anything I ever wrote. It all had to happen as it did, so what is there to question?

I Love you,

I AM, Wayne

In this email to his friend, our dad wrote the words that we'd all been pondering: "I am entering a new phase in my life." This trip to Australia and his meeting Maithri was not his final trip there—he visited again two years later with Saje and Skye—but the time he spent in Australia giving his lectures and the weeks and months leading up to it were a time of great suffering for him, as his neck pain was basically unbearable. Still, in the midst of all of that, he could recognize that in his quest for reaching the highest rung on the ladder that is placed before each of us upon the moment of our birth, divine love, learning and teaching, and mastering it was the new phase he was entering, what ultimately would be his last phase in his physical body. For after you reach the highest rung: *That's where the ladder's rungs come to a stop and there are no more objects comprised of particles. It's pure energy manifested as love.*

This is what Hafiz was explaining in his poem "In a Treehouse" that our dad mentioned in the email to his friend. Serena found a version translated by Daniel Ladinsky[1] and marveled over the message contained in the lines:

> Light
> will someday split you open
> even if your life is now a cage,
>
> For a divine seed, the crown of destiny,
> is hidden and sown on an ancient, fertile plain
> that you hold the title to.
>
> Love will surely bust you wide open
> into an unfettered, blooming new galaxy
> A life-giving radiance will come,
>
> O look again within yourself,
> For I know you were once the elegant host
> To all the marvels in creation.
>
> From a sacred crevice in your body,
> a bow rises each night
> and shoots your soul into God.
>
> Behold the Beautiful One
> from the vantage point of Love.
>
> He is conducting the affairs
> of the whole universe
> in a tree house—on a limb
> in your heart.

She reread the email and the Hafiz poem over and over again. As she did, she felt a true shift take place within her. It became clear to her that her father had the Knowing that his true purpose in life was to reach pure divine love and leave a trail for others to follow and learn for themselves . . . and that's what he did. Rereading his words about his "next phase" inspired Serena to focus less on worldly things—goals and external achievements—and instead to become one with the Divine, to find her own *Shibumi*. Her life led her to this Knowing that the bad times, the court cases, challenges with motherhood and marriage, and the heartache over the loss of our dad and Mason are places where love and beauty can enter and "bust her wide open into an unfettered, blooming new galaxy." She has a deep faith—the Knowing—that her father wouldn't have left his children if he didn't know in his heart that they could handle life on their own.

Our dad was a man who lived a life of service, a life of learning, so that he could then teach. He lived a life in which he came to know that he was reaching the final rung of his own ladder, the final phase of his life, and that what lay beyond was a world no longer comprised of physical particles that many of us falsely identify as our true purpose. Dad realized that the true purpose of his incarnation was to teach pure, divine love and leave a trail for all of us who come after him to learn for ourselves as well.

Once Serena understood this, she could clearly look back and see how many of her conflicts, anxieties, and even goals had been full of decisions that were not love focused but ego driven. Her energy had been spent on amassing wealth, reputation, accomplishment, and getting her body and home—her life—set up in a way that seemed perfect. Hafiz said that "Light will some-day split you open even if your life is now a cage." She could look back and see that all the struggles and con-flicts that had arisen in her life were simply Life's way of splitting her open so the Divine could enter. Her sense of love and worth was derived from the love she shared with family and friends, while her soul continued to align with experiences that challenged her to let go of the "marvels of creation" and, instead, to return to the place within herself that is pure love, the place where God resides—the Knowing. She wanted to become a host to God, consumed with the love one experiences when they are operating from a God-realized place and no longer the slave of the ego.

Her entire life had been leading her to this moment, to the Knowing that the wounds were necessary so the light could slip in. When she finally learned to get out of her own way, she found herself in the express lane of the highway, in the driver's seat of her own vehicle filled with all the people who appeared in life to teach her what she needed to learn in this lifetime. What bumps and roadblocks she'll encounter along the way still remain to be seen, but this time around, she can be certain that remaining a host to God, serving others, and, most importantly, allowing the highest part of herself to be free to experience life as it is, rather than clinging to what she thinks it should be, will make all the difference in enjoy-ing the ride.

Serena began to apply this lesson daily, especially after her experience of Matt's legal issues. It seemed that the more she adopted this, the more the legal issues became an oft-forgotten background narrative that no longer had control over how she experienced life. She began to feel that whatever will be will be, but in the meantime, she could seek the highest form of love and acceptance that was possible for her, the place of complete and total surrender.

> I'd bought into the idea that when all the pieces in my life fell into place, then I'd be able to start, then I'd be worthy of offering a message, but it's the other way around: when I have peace, which only I can create for myself, everything else will shift. Not if everything shifts, then I'll have peace. I get that lesson so often, but then I lose it . . . then get it again.

THE GUIDING FORCE

Once again, we saw through our father's example that some of his greatest gifts are not what he told us but what he showed us—his determination to not die with his music still in him (as he so often said), even though he sometimes missed family and school events because he was working for the greater good and living his dreams. This balances our mom's example—her dharma is to be a mother, and she's made that her vocation, both with her immediate family and by offering her nurturing energy to anyone who needs it. We have a Knowing that we can be and do all these things—writing and speaking and mothering and sharing our truth—as we bring our music into the world.

Many themes have come up for us during the writing of this book, and when we look back on the years that led up to this, we can see clearly that there was always a guiding force that offered wisdom and peace in the midst of the chaos, pain, or struggles, but it could only appear when we allowed it. Allowing is like surrendering, which we have written about extensively in these last few chapters. Allowing is the same as recognizing that each of us contains that insular Tahiti, a piece of paradise that exists within us that no one can take from us no matter what the external circumstances of our lives look like. But in order to access it, we must allow ourselves to remember that at any given time, we can choose peace. The inner place of peace is ours and ours alone, and when we completely allow ourselves to go there, whether through meditation, silence, prayer, or consciously replacing thoughts of fear with thoughts of love, we experience ultimate freedom.

As our dad used to say, "What you resist persists." What you focus on, even if it is not something you want, you draw into your life. What you resist persists, because when you resist something, you create a counterforce to what it is that you are desiring. As Newton's third law of motion states: "When one body exerts a force on a second body, the second body simultaneously exerts a force equal in magnitude and opposite in direction on the first body." In other words, for every action, there is an equal and opposite reaction. Thoughts, like everything else in the universe, are made of energy, and therefore, Newton's law could also be reframed as "For every thought you have, there is an equal and opposite thought that you also create." Our dad used to remind us to choose our thoughts wisely, for what we focus on, whether it is something we want or don't want, we ultimately call into our lives.

When we make it a habit of living from our own inner Tahiti, we reaffirm to the universe that what we want more of is peace, and when we use meditation to hone that skill of slowing down our thoughts or replacing thoughts of what we don't want with thoughts of what we do, we become in complete synchronization with the flow of the universe. When we were children, the Prayer of Saint Francis or the "Peace Prayer" served as a reminder of this universal secret.

> Lord, make me an instrument of thy peace!
> That where there is hatred, I may bring love.
> That where there is wrong, I may bring the spirit
>   of forgiveness.
> That where there is discord, I may bring harmony.
> That where there is error, I may bring truth.
> That where there is doubt, I may bring faith.
> That where there is despair, I may bring hope.
> That where there are shadows, I may bring light.
> That where there is sadness, I may bring joy.
> Lord, grant that I may seek rather to comfort,
>   than to be comforted.
> To understand, than to be understood.
> To love, than to be loved.
> For it is by self-forgetting that one finds.
> It is by forgiving that one is forgiven.
> It is by dying that one awakens to Eternal Life.[2]

In other words (and if our thoughts make up the majority of the energy we put out), we get what we think about, whether it is what we *want* or not. It is easy to become slightly obsessed with self-correcting our thoughts, especially when we first set out to put this into practice, but ultimately, the greatest ability we have in receiving what it is we are seeking comes from our ability to think about it, imagine it, and surrender to what comes while always making a point of revisiting that inner place of ultimate peace. Let go of the package you think it should come in, let go of the time frame you have placed on receiving, and simply let God do the rest. Herein is your Knowing.

A Way of Knowing

Pay attention to the green lights.

After our dad's death, we experienced glimpses of Knowing at first, but it got to a point where we found ourselves constantly living in that space. Our dad used to close his letters by saying, "I send you love and only green lights." And that's what we want for ourselves, for our children, for you, for everyone—*love and only green lights*. When we're flowing with the green lights, we're on a path to surrendering. Surrender the attachment you have to how things must be in order to have peace. Remind yourself that peace is available to you in every moment, and it will not come from something or someone else. Experiencing peace, or flowing with the universe rather than against it, can only come from within. Getting all green lights is another way of describing what happens when you are in harmony with yourself and therefore with the universe.

Peace cannot exist where there is conflict, and if you have a mind at war with itself, you will not experience the feeling, the Knowing, of God's presence. When your mind is at war with itself, when you live a lie, constantly condemn yourself, or perpetuate habits that take you away from where you want to be, you take yourself further away from being in alignment with your highest self. Your highest self, the part of you that is God, only wants to feel good. If you are doing things that don't make you feel good, or if you are allowing your mind to think thoughts that tear you apart, you are perpetuating the exact negative energy you don't want in your life. When you pretend to be someone you are not or do things that are not in harmony with who you would like to be, your mind becomes a war zone, for when you are not in harmony with your highest self, you will find yourself living a life of conflict. If you seem to be attracting conflict everywhere you go, ask yourself, "Is what I am doing and what I am thinking in harmony with who I would like to be?" Throughout our lives, we will find ourselves facing obstacles or difficulties along the way, but it is in choosing how we respond to these obstacles or difficulties that we will find our ultimate freedom.

If we accept the maxim to be true that conflict cannot survive without our participation, then we must consider the role we are playing in the conflicts that arise in our lives. When Serena was experiencing one difficult situation after the other and peace seemed unattainable, she had to remind herself over and over that her mind was convincing her that once everything fell into place, she could then experience peace. This is an example of the mind being at war with itself. The mind, when left unchecked, will run wild with thoughts that place the answers to our problems outside ourselves. True wisdom is in knowing that the peace we seek is available at any moment, but we must go within to find it. Rather than believing that everything must fall into place in order for us to have peace, which takes away the greatest power you have been given, remind yourself over and over that first you must find your own peace within, and then everything will fall into place. This is the key to creating the life you desire and to getting yourself back into the flow of the universe, where the green lights are always facing your direction.

One of the greatest lessons Serena learned during her entire experience with her husband's legal ordeal (which is ongoing) is that she so often feared the absolute worst would happen, and she spent so much time being afraid of what might happen that the precious time she had at home with her husband and children went by in a blur.

It is as though she was terrified of him having to go to prison, but instead of really enjoying and marinating in the joy of being at home with her family intact, she focused instead on what it would be like in his absence.

We all do this, but how often do we stop to really take in the present moment, really notice the weight of our children on our laps, the way they look first thing in the morning or the sound their laughter makes? How often do we spend our precious currency in this lifetime, which is our time, focused on what we don't want to happen rather than appreciating what we currently have and soaking it all in? We mentioned before that it is important to choose your thoughts wisely, but even more so, it is crucial to soak in the moments that you so desired and really immerse yourself in extreme gratitude for the moments that are easy, beautiful, and simple. Time will pass by quickly, and in a blink of an eye, your once-newborn is now five and waving to you as she enters her kindergarten classroom; your youthful body transitions to a more "lived-in" version; the seasons change and the sun continues to set, until one day, you are taking your final breath on this earth.

But really ask yourself, will you stay present enough to give a silent thank-you each and every day you are alive on this earth? If you make a commitment to starting today, you might find that you are aware of just how precious time is. To spend your time in conflict with others, with your circumstances, or with yourself is like filling your home with furniture you despise. Our thoughts are the currency we have in this lifetime, and what we spend our thoughts on is not only what we fill our minds with but what our life ends up becoming. Some people spend their entire lives fearing the worst, constantly in a state of worry or anxiety over things that never come to pass, but they end up living a life full of fear, which blocks out the love they instead could be experiencing. The more you express gratitude in the present moment, the more you will find yourself soaking up each and every passing day, no longer wasting your thoughts and energy on everything that could go wrong.

If you have spent every day up until this point criticizing or condemning yourself or others, take a moment to observe the way that makes you feel. Does participating in inner conflict bring you joy or peace or remind you of how loved you are? The answer is no. Your highest self not only wants peace, it is peace. Every time you find yourself in a conflict with yourself or someone else or find yourself out of flow with the green lights the universe is wanting to send you, remind yourself that you too have your own inner Tahiti. We do not measure our spiritual growth by the number of difficult situations that arise in our lives but instead by how we find ourselves responding to these difficulties or conflicts. Do we respond with love or fear? What you choose will set the course for whether you move into the flow of the universe or against it. You can choose to see the light in even the darkest of places by finding your inner Tahiti and consciously redirecting your thoughts to that space. It is from there that you will become in alignment with all the green lights the universe has to offer.

CHAPTER 10

The Path of Least Resistance

"By surrendering, you create an energy field
of receptivity for the solution to appear."

DR. WAYNE W. DYER,
THE POWER OF INTENTION

I HOPE YOU DANCE

Our dad loved to find lessons everywhere—in potted plants or the grocery store and many places in between. Once, when Saje was with our dad in the car, the song "I Hope You Dance" began to play on the radio. As they listened, he told her he agreed with every statement in the lyrics—from never losing a sense of wonder to never fearing those mountains in the distance—except for one. Then he asked her, "Can you figure out which it is?"

Saje paid careful attention as Lee Ann Womack sang of taking chances and not taking things for granted, and when she'd finished, Saje and our dad discussed many of the verses in the song. He finally revealed the one line he did not feel was good advice: "Never settle for the path of least resistance." He believed you should *always* take the path of least resistance, because when the universe is offering opposition or putting hindrances in front of you, it's for a reason, even though you may not be able to understand it at the time.

To stop resisting is to surrender. To be clear, surrendering does not mean giving up. It does not mean quitting. Surrendering is far more beautiful, more meaningful. It connotes letting go of the attachment to the way you think things ought to be so you can move into the beauty of experiencing things as they are. We can become consumed with the belief that we can control life's events through our own limited mindset, but this is an attempt to control the uncontrollable, and we get stuck in the way we think things should be, which often prevents us from receiving blessings as they come. Consider that your failure or breakup or job loss might be a gift, bringing you one step closer to where you *really* want to be. When this Knowing happens, you align with miracles.

This connects to what we've been saying about synchronicities and yielding to the signs, because when you are in the flow, close to your Knowing, you see and experience a smoother path as circumstances fall into place, the right people come into your life, or the one thing you really need shows up. On the other hand, if you are experiencing a great deal of struggle when it's not serving you or others, this is likely a time to surrender—to step back and take a good look at whatever it is you are worrying about, holding on to, or trying to achieve—and ask if this is the highest and best thing for you and the people around you. When you do, a whole new path of possibilities will open to you. Surrendering is saying yes to the universe. It makes way for allowing your desires to flow to you effortlessly.

A CUP OF PROBLEMS

Serena knows a thing or two about traveling the path of *most* resistance. Shortly after she and Matt got married, she began to express to him her deep desire to live on Maui. It is a special place for our whole family. It was where our dad had spent much of his time, and she'd always felt at home there. When she became pregnant with her first daughter, Sailor, the longing to move to Hawaii became even stronger. She visualized Matt and herself raising their children there, creating the perfect home.

Then, in 2015, her world fell apart. Three months after Sailor was born, Matt was indicted, and three months after that, our dad died. The dream of Maui was obscured by her grief and the terror of losing their savings and everything they owned. Throughout the process of Matt's five-year legal battle, these possibilities became even less of a reality. The stress was all-consuming as Serena chose to resist life as it was unfolding. It was a fight for her to surrender to circumstances that were out of her control anyway—the accusations had been made, the legal system operated in its own time, and she couldn't undo the past. She was so driven by fear that she rarely allowed herself to accept what was happening and trust that the universe really did have her back, that this experience was bringing her closer to where she was meant to be. On a more spiritual level, perhaps this entire legal crisis was something she needed as an opportunity to grow, to evolve, to learn the true meaning of the art of letting go.

Her reluctance to put her faith in the spiritual truth that the universe could serve her and challenge her in ways that brought her closer to where she was destined to go in this lifetime was based in her fear of the unknown. When the pain became too much to bear, Serena finally asked herself, "How long am I willing to resist the present because I am afraid of an imagined future?" Surrender was the *only* thing that could bring her closer to where she really wanted to be in life. Were her anxiety and fatalistic thinking—about losing her home, about what would happen to her child if her husband went to prison—serving her? Of course not. Dad used to say, "Go out and find me a cup of problems." You can't pick up anxiety and put it in a cup—it's your desire to perceive life as you think it ought to be, rather than breathing through what currently is, that creates the anxiety.

Once again, this brings to mind the passage in Herman Melville's *Moby Dick* our dad loved so very much, the one we read at his celebration of life: "For as this appalling ocean surrounds the verdant land, so in the soul of man there lies one insular Tahiti, full of peace and joy, but encompassed by all the horrors of the half-known life."[1] Serena recognized that although she had a longing for a life on Maui—a beautiful area, her dream home, her family just as she pictured it—Maui was just an outward symbol of the insular Tahiti she sought. After three years of resisting her father's death and then Mason's as well (which were things that could not be undone) and resisting her husband's legal battle (which was something that was out of her hands) and resisting losing her home and money (which was again outside her control), she came to an acceptance of her life just as it was. She could find her insular Tahiti amid every challenge she was experiencing in Florida.

How many times have we heard someone we admire—a successful or joyful person—say something like, "Had I been given the job I thought I really wanted, I never would have ended up getting to where I am now, which is the place I was ultimately meant to be." Or, "Had I stayed in the relationship I fought so hard to make work, I never would have ended up meeting the love of my life." How often do we fight to hold onto something that does not serve us, something that keeps us limited in our experience? Only when Serena began to recognize that her resistance was based in fear was she able to begin the process of complete surrender.

When we were growing up, our dad loved to tell a story about a man devoted to his religion who had a strong belief in God. One day, the man was lost at sea and drowning. He called out to God, "Please! I have been a faithful servant of yours for many years—please save me!" Suddenly, a piece of driftwood floated up to him, large enough for the man to sit on, but he ignored it, because he was convinced God would come and save him. Again, the man asked, "God, please save me!" A ship sailed by, but rather than shout for help, the man remained convinced only God could save him. With his last breath, the man begged God to rescue him, and a lifeguard appeared with a kayak, urging the man to climb in. But the man resisted, waiting for God to show up. The man drowned. When he arrived in heaven, he asked, "God, why did you not send a miracle to save me? I was your faithful servant, but you did not rescue me when I needed you." God looked at the man and said, "What the hell do you think the driftwood, the ship, and the lifeguard were?"

The miracle is not the driftwood, ship, or lifeguard. The miracle is *recognizing* that the driftwood is your chance to save your own life. It is understanding that the best path out of your troubles is there if you pay attention. It is changing your perspective on what is happening so you are present enough in each moment to understand that everything you perceive as a crisis can also be a chance for growth, for your soul's evolution. A miracle is what you experience when you surrender to life as it is.

Serena still doesn't know if she will move to Maui this year or next year or in ten years. She does know she can choose to view her troubles as lessons rather than obstacles. When she does, miracles appear, like when she spotted the "Mason" license plate reminding her to "Let there be light" and moments later Matt's attorney called to say the prosecution had admitted corruption before and during the trial.

Each day Serena was not on Maui, she had to find Maui within—her insular Tahiti—through the process of complete and total surrender. That is exactly what she did, and it saved her from a lifetime of drowning in uncontrollable circumstance. Through a conscious process of letting go, of giving up on resistance, we can begin to view each loss or crisis as a gift, a piece of driftwood, rarely packaged or presented in the way we would have chosen yet exactly what we need to get closer to where our soul, our ultimate highest self, needs to be. You don't have a say in everything that happens to you. However, you do have a say in whether you allow yourself to be consumed by crises and losses or be transformed by them. The only things you can control in life are your actions.

I AM WILLING TO SEE
THIS DIFFERENTLY

The Christmas before he passed away, our dad sent everyone in our family a DVD recording of a program he'd done with Esther Hicks, who channels a group of spiritual beings collectively known as Abraham. After Esther's husband, Jerry, had died, Esther was grief-stricken, and although she is someone who is able to communicate with the "other side," she was unable to connect with her partner of many years. On the recording, Abraham explained that Esther was so focused on her previous connection with Jerry in the physical realm that she lost sight of being able to connect with him in the spirit world, despite this being her gift, a gift she and Jerry had shared.

Serena was struck by the realization that it was only when Esther yielded to the Knowing that although Jerry had passed away and she was full of grief, she needed to return to the love they shared to experience him where he now was. Once she shifted her memories of him to those of love instead of sadness, she was able to connect with him again. She had to elevate her own energy in order to reach the energy of where Jerry was now operating from, the energy of love. She couldn't reach him when she was operating from grief, but in returning to love, she found him again.

After receiving the call saying our father had died, Serena thought about that DVD and knew that if she wanted to stay connected with our father, she had to return to the place of joy, love, and peace inside herself where he could reach her—where his soul is now. The moment she was able to surrender to what was, to accept that his death wasn't going to be undone, the closer she was to contentment. It seemed odd that she had to let go of him as she knew him to get closer to him now, but the more she released the desire to have what was, the more she was able to experience his love in the present moment. When she stopped trying to hold on to the physical person he had been, she was able to experience the love he felt for her as his daughter and she felt for him as her father. The same thing happened after Mason passed away. In the moments before drifting off to sleep, when she was able to remember a really happy moment they had shared, she then had that powerful dream in which he appeared to her, bathed in light, smiling and laughing and letting her know that he loved her, and she knew she loved him and that none of the other petty dramas between them mattered.

Whenever we have a major loss or crisis in our life, the immediate reaction is to want things to revert to the way they were, but the more you cling to the past, the more stress you experience in the present. Allowing life to occur as it will rather than how we think it should be can liberate us to experience the joy of the present moment. Our dad used to say we should all strive to have a mind that is open to everything and attached to nothing. When we surrender, we experience far more miraculous events than when we resist life's flow.

Picture it like this: What if you moved into a beautiful new house, your dream home, and a benefactor gave you unlimited funds to furnish it? Would you fill it with furniture you hated—uncomfortable, useless, or reminding you of something or someone you'd rather forget?

Of course not. Your mind is like that house, and your thoughts are your currency. You can spend your currency on thoughts you do not want or even like very much, or you can spend it on things that encourage growth, comfort, happiness. It's up to you. When you connect to your Knowing, you realize your thoughts are up to you—they are your creation.

A LITTLE "OFF"

When our friend Avianna Castro asked Saje to come to a spiritual retreat she was leading on Maui and not only be her guest but also speak to the other participants, Saje excitedly agreed. Although Saje often experienced some nerves before giving a talk, in the past, she had always been able to calm them by creating an outline. It gave her the sense of control she needed and allowed her to feel excitement for the talk.

When Saje arrived in Maui a few days before the event, she met with Avianna to discuss logistics. To her surprise, one of the first things Avianna said was, "I don't want you to plan anything. Whatever your heart feels will be right in that moment." She wanted Saje's talk to flow from the universe, and she asked all her speakers to forego any outlines or preparation and instead surrender to what was meant to be when they got up on stage.

Saje's immediate thought was, "That's okay; I can memorize my outline, so no worries there." But as the days passed and the time for her talk approached, she began to consider Avianna's request. After much deliberation, she decided to honor Avianna's wishes, even though speaking to a large group without a plan was outside her comfort zone. After all, it was Avianna's event. Instead of staying stuck in outline mode, Saje decided she would stop and say a prayer of surrender, asking God to take the reins and guide her as she spoke so she could be of the highest service to the people attending the talk. She prayed for confidence, saying the prayer she has come to rely on: "God, I am willing to see this differently." This wasn't always easy and often took a great deal of effort, especially as the date got closer and her anxiety kicked in, but she continued to say this prayer and to relinquish her control over how the talk should go.

When the big moment arrived, Saje took the stage at the venue without an outline or a single note. She hadn't been lazy or unprepared for something she had signed up for. However, she trusted in her ability to connect to the infinite wisdom available to all of us—her Knowing. Unexpectedly, as she began to speak, she felt a deep calm. She was far calmer than usual, and she gave a talk that surprised her. Stories spilled out effortlessly, and her ability to offer what she had learned was clearer than anything before—she'd never given a better talk in her life. The audience members were visibly moved; some wept, and most wiped tears from their eyes. Saje was amazed.

When we were kids, our dad framed a quote and hung it on the wall of our family home. It said, "Good morning. This is God. I will be handling all your problems today. I will not need your help, so have a miraculous day." Letting God handle Saje's talk at Avianna's event opened her eyes to the benefits of this mystery of surrendering and flowing.

What Saje learned from giving this talk was really put to the test the following summer. Most of our family was back in Maui, and there were lots of children there. Serena was pregnant with her son, Forrest, Sailor was three, and Windsor was about to turn two. And Skye was there with her son Waylen, who was nine months old. Not to mention all of our friends out in Maui who have small children. Saje loved being an aunt, but living in such close quarters with all those little children confirmed her conviction to wait to have a baby. It wasn't that she didn't love every minute spent with the munchkins, but she also enjoyed being able to head out to the beach without having to put sunscreen on two other people, bring snacks and floaties and drinks, and then find a bathroom ASAP. She experienced firsthand the freedoms you lose when you become a parent, and she knew she wasn't quite ready for that.

Even though Saje's husband had expressed on many occasions that he was more than ready for a baby whenever she was, she told Anthony she wanted another year, and they could reassess then. They had been having a wonderful time as newlyweds, and Saje was traveling all over the world and enjoying being a twenty-nine-year-old in New York City, and she wasn't ready to give that up yet. Not to mention, in her mind, they were not financially secure enough to start a family. Her time with her nieces and nephew was all the nicer, because she knew in a couple short weeks, she'd go back to having nonstop peace and quiet, where the only person she had to concern herself with was herself. And selfishly, she thought this sounded pretty great.

Saje's plans for herself, Anthony, and her future family came to a halt before she got back to New York. She felt a little "off" and hadn't really given it much thought at first—it was probably the effects of traveling and vacation food. But at around three o'clock one morning, she woke up in a panic—she had a Knowing that she was pregnant, and she was certain she was expecting a baby boy. An odd yet powerful feeling had come over her, and there was no denying it. The idea of being pregnant did not instantly lead to feelings of elation or excitement but instead, if she was being completely honest, to feelings of dread, fear, and panic. After several minutes of going down a rabbit hole of negativity, she convinced herself she was being crazy, that she had absolutely no evidence she was pregnant, and she should go back to sleep and forget about all of this. Eventually, she did.

She woke up early the next morning and decided to take a pregnancy test (even though she was still a couple days away from a missed period). Luckily, she had a lot of them. When Serena had found out she was pregnant with Forrest a couple months earlier, she'd put all her unused tests in Saje's travel bag, promising Saje would certainly need them before Serena ever would again. (Three kids in three years can do this to you.)

Saje unwrapped one of the tests and peed on it without much concern, convinced it would confirm she was being silly and was not pregnant, like every other month of her life. However, it was only a matter of seconds before her fear began to escalate as she saw the two lines forming simultaneously. Her hands were shaking . . . she was pregnant. She knew she should be happy. She knew this was a miracle.

A soul had chosen her to be its mom, and she should feel honored and excited. But she didn't. All she could think about was how much her life was going to change and how she didn't welcome the changes.

Serena had a different reaction: she was ecstatic, giddy with delight. Just the day before, Saje had said she wanted children but was happy waiting and enjoying her new marriage. Serena often joked that her daughters didn't know who their actual mother was—Saje or Serena—such was Saje's presence in their lives. Serena was also excited by the idea of being pregnant at the same time as her sister, having babies who would share the same milestones, as close as cousins can get.

Saje spent the day sharing her news with immediate family and pretended to take part in the delight everyone else expressed. Anthony was the most thrilled of all, albeit a little shocked, because they weren't quite sure when this could have happened. For the sake of everyone, particularly Anthony, she put on a happy face and went through the motions, but inside, she was feeling terrible and then, on top of that, guilty. Because this was her child who she would be bringing into this world, and it didn't seem right to feel anything but joy—after all, she'd always wanted a baby, just not quite yet. Not to mention, she kept telling herself there were so many people out there who struggled and struggled to get pregnant, and she was taking her miracle for granted.

It didn't matter; she couldn't be happy. All she could think about was how in eight months, life as she'd known it would be over. She would never travel unencumbered again; she would have nothing in common with the majority of her friends, who didn't have kids yet; she and Anthony would have to move out of New York because they couldn't afford a two-bedroom apartment; she'd have to stop pursuing any type of career; and on and on her negative thoughts escalated.

That night, our brother-in-law Mo asked Saje how she was feeling, and she broke down in tears in the middle of our family dinner. She got honest with everyone about how scared she was and then how ashamed she felt for having these feelings. Sharing her heart with the people she loved helped a little, but it still didn't stop her thoughts.

Saje stayed in this place of regret, fear, and guilt for a few weeks. Life had handed her some new circumstances, and no matter how she responded to them or framed them, her baby would arrive. But as the days wore on and she grew weary of this frame of mind, she realized once again that she did have a choice. She could go on telling herself how her life as she knew it was over and continue fear-based thoughts about how terrible things would be, or she could choose to surrender. Once again, she prayed: "Dear God, I am willing to see this differently."

This decision to see things differently began to make all the difference. She allowed herself to bring into her consciousness thoughts of all the joy and love this new life would bring, whereas before, she had been closed off to these thoughts and ideas. This change in perception gradually changed her pregnancy to a joyous one of excitement and celebration, as opposed to the doomsday countdown it had felt like before.

Saje is further down the road of parenthood now, adores her beautiful son unconditionally, and already feels she's learned and grown a lot, which she's confident will multiply infinitely as time goes on. But just like Serena did with the legal troubles and finding her insular Tahiti, Saje will always remember that the understanding and growth don't begin until you surrender to God's greater plan. Our dad taught us in so many ways to become aware that there are no accidents in our intelligent universe. Realize everything that shows up has something to teach you. Appreciate everything and everyone in your life. We've come to trust, when we're experiencing resistance, that it might be a reason to sit back and take a good look at what we're trying to achieve and ask if it is the highest and best thing for us and the people we love.

GUARDIAN ANGEL

Sometimes a sign can be pretty tangible, like a feather or a parking spot. Sometimes it can be waking up with a powerful and certain Knowing. Or it can be as mystical as the guardian angel that guided our mom during the birth of her first baby. When she was pregnant with her first child, she had only heard that childbirth involved extreme suffering and extreme pain and that everybody should take the drugs and numb themselves so they didn't feel anything. She was so desirous of being a mother—her career path was to be a mother—that she didn't want to be absent during the birth of her baby. She prayed, asking that she be wide awake with wonder, allowed to witness the birth of her child without any drugs.

What happened to her was beyond her wildest imagination, her wildest dream. Her water broke at 2:00 a.m., and twenty minutes later, she was at the hospital, having her first contraction. She grabbed the rails in pain as a nurse told her she was half a centimeter dilated, which was a long way from the ten centimeters she had to get to. She didn't know if she could make it. Then a pretty nurse dressed in blue with auburn hair came to her bedside, and our mom asked her, "How can I get through this labor?"

She pulled all our mom's long hair back behind the pillow and put her hand on Mom's forehead, and she said, "There is a place within you to breathe. Go there now, and you will not suffer."

When our mom opened her eyes, it was four in the morning. She hit the call button, because she felt a huge surge of energy and knew she was ready to have her baby. The nurses arrived and didn't agree. Something was weird. Our mom hadn't screamed in labor; she'd been asleep. So how could she be dilated? Our mom was positive, and when they gave in and checked, there was her baby's head, crowning and ready to emerge.

The doctor arrived, and Mom told him she had only had one contraction and didn't feel any more, so could she push? He looked at the nurses and asked, "What did you give her?" And they said, "Nothing. She's been asleep." While they were deliberating, our mom pushed her baby into the world. It was one of the highlights of her life then and each of the six other times she did so, but this experience was unique, because after her healthy child was delivered, a nurse came over to her and said, "Everybody's talking about you. What did you experience in your birth? We've never had an experience like yours, with only one contraction."

Our mom told her about the encounter with the nurse with the auburn hair and the blue dress. The other nurse shook her head and walked away, coming back a few minutes later with two other nurses. She told Mom, "We've been in labor and delivery, all of us, for over thirteen years. And the person you described does not work here."

Mom surrendered to her Knowing and was given something that was beyond time and space. That kind of experience allowed her to have no fear for the rest of her six births despite numerous contractions. No matter how one chooses to interpret signs, they're a universal reminder to pay attention and follow the path of least resistance.

SURRENDER TO THE KNOWING

We've come to realize that when we're experiencing resistance, it might be a reason to sit back and take a good look at what we're trying to achieve and ask if it is the highest and best thing for us and the people we love. When you are in the flow, in harmony with the universe, and have connected to the Knowing, you'll find confirmations along the way. Your path will be smooth, the right people will come into your life, and fear and anxiety will be replaced by hope and peace as you surrender to God's greater plan.

When you want something, when you seek something, when you force the universe, you are not a vibrational match, because wanting means there's a lack or gap between you and what you desire. Our dad used to say that *The Secret* got it wrong. In life, you don't get what you want; you get what you are. Nothing is missing. The Knowing is about surrendering, receiving, and transforming.

A Way of Knowing

Surrender everything—
intentionally—and let God.

As we have gotten older, we have come to realize that when we ask the universe how we may serve rather than focusing on our own suffering or grief, the universe conspires to serve us as well. More times than we can count, we have had people say that *The Power of Intention* was the most life-changing book they have ever read. For some people, it has even become a life manual. Little do they know it was written during the darkest storm of our father's life.

During the first weeks of the summer during which our parents were on the path to divorce, our dad had stopped writing and reading and was swallowed up in grief. Slowly, we encouraged him to get back to writing, and eventually, he did. It was his desire to use his suffering, his personal struggle, as an opportunity to become even more compassionate, more connected with his readers, and ultimately with the inner calling of his soul, which was urging him to draw from this experience and then teach, that allowed him to find the strength in the midst of the pain. That strength, or once again, that U-turn to his higher self, his inner Knowing, was what got him through the storm.

He poured himself into his work, and the result was a book called *The Power of Intention*.

Written during one of the most difficult times in his life, that book went on to sell more than a million copies, helping countless people during *their* most difficult times. When our dad was able to focus on his work, on how he could use his suffering to help people, his experience began to change. It was magnificent to watch him focus on serving others with his writing and his teaching. While doing so, the experience of his separation from our mom began to change.

Dad's focus shifted from himself and all the pain and self-pity he was experiencing to one of channeling his emotions toward service to others and his life's work. Doing this allowed him to have a true understanding for our Mom's decision and even compassion toward her. This compassion led him to treat her with kindness instead of judgment and resentment. Our dad often reminded us of the saying used in twelve-step programs: "There are no justified resentments." When he stopped blaming and resenting Mom for her actions, understanding that she was justified in wanting to move on, his love for her resurfaced, because after all, love does not judge. This led to them firing the attorneys and realizing they could conduct their marriage on their own terms.

Likewise, once our mom put her focus back on her children and on remaining loving and forgiving of our father, her life experience changed as well. She went on to meet a great man who is still a part of our family to this day, a man our dad came to know and have a friendship with—all of which seemed impossible when the divorce conversation first began.

The experience of having our parents begin the process of getting divorced then call it off and decide to remain married, but on their own terms, became the foundation for how we thought of marriage and relationships in general. Our parents being married but seeing other people and living separately seemed bizarre to outsiders, and we often received awkward questions about their situation. But the longer it went on, the more comfortable—proud, even—we were as we explained that this was what worked for them. They were doing marriage *their* way, and it wasn't up to anyone else to define what it looked like or meant for them. When we were young women, this felt liberating. Once again, we realized that life was not happening to us, it was responding to us, and we could decide to become victims of our circumstances and stay resentful toward either of our parents for the new family dynamic, *or* we could process life as it was rather than how we thought it was supposed to be.

Disappointment so often stems from an attachment to an outcome or an expectation of how we think things ought to be that when we remain glued to the expectation, we fail to experience life as it *is*. In choosing to accept the way their relationship evolved, we were able to free ourselves from negative, lingering feelings that got in the way of our own sense of peace. More important, it freed us from having to remain committed to hurt feelings directed at our parents, which required much more work and stress than choosing to let it go and find the beauty in the new "marriage" our parents adopted.

As we were growing up, our parents taught us that remaining committed to "justified resentment" would only hurt us in the long run and only lead to more suffering, and who wants that? It's what Anne Lamott meant when she wrote, "Holding onto a resentment was like eating rat poison and waiting for the rat to die."[2] Our dad often said that there are no justified resentments, because there is nothing in the world that would justify choosing to feel committed to anything other than peace. Remaining committed to your resentments takes away the ability to experience peace, and as we often heard as children, at any time, we can choose peace rather than this feeling.

Our highest selves, the part of us that is connected to all living things, wants peace—that is the Knowing. When we align ourselves with thoughts and feelings of peace, of joy, of connection, we become a vibrational match to what it is we are seeking. When we focus on how we've been wronged, how unfair life is, or why our life's circumstances are not our fault, we not only take away our own ability to align with peace, abundance, and love, but more egregiously, we take away our ability to become the directors of our own lives. As Oprah Winfrey put it in the finale of her television talk show, "Nobody but you is responsible for your life. It doesn't matter what your mama did; it doesn't matter what your daddy didn't do. You are responsible for your life. . . . You are responsible for the energy that you create for yourself, and you're responsible for the energy that you bring to others."[3] How freeing is that?

Our friend and mentor, Gabrielle Bernstein, has a deck of "Super Attractor" cards that we love, and we often pull one out for inspiration or when we feel stuck and are asking the universe for guidance. As Serena explains, "One of the cards that really stuck with me said, 'My greatest spiritual shifts don't come through force, they come through freedom.'" When you remain attached to your resentments or the feeling of having been wronged by someone, you stay in the energy of that wrong and therefore align with more of it. When you operate from the place of knowing, you truly understand that it is in your best interest to let it all go. Just let it go.

If you aren't in a place of wanting to forgive, you can still release yourself from the hold that the resentment or anger has on you. If you find that you would like to forgive whoever hurt you or whatever wrong you have experienced but don't know how, remind yourself that your anger is what is keeping you prisoner. It is what ties you to the very thing you want to let go of. If you feel that whoever hurt you is not deserving of your forgiveness, understand that the only one suffering from your lack of forgiveness is you. No one else lives inside your head. It is you who feels the pain of the resentment and no one else. If it is your own self that needs forgiving, write down the words of the brilliant Maya Angelou and repeat them throughout your day: "Forgive yourself for not knowing what you didn't know before you learned it."[4]

CHAPTER 11

Especially Love

"I end on love no matter what."
DR. WAYNE W. DYER,
*CHANGE YOUR THOUGHTS
—CHANGE YOUR LIFE*

A HEART EXPANDING BEYOND THE SELF

Saje spent much of her pregnancy in denial that she was having a baby. You wouldn't have known this from her behavior; she certainly took good care of herself and planned for her child. She had a baby shower and set up a nursery and took birthing classes. She went through all the motions, but in some sense, she was in denial that her son was actually arriving. She never once dreamt about having a baby or being a mother, and she felt that was proof of her denial. She wasn't unhappy or scared, at least that she was aware of; it was more as if her mind had put a block on what was to come. For some reason, she felt small and almost unworthy of parenthood.

At her doctor's appointments, she never wanted to take up too much space. Although Saje had a good idea of what she wanted as far as her birth plan, she never brought it up to her doctor and had a strong awareness of not wanting to seem needy. At the end of each appointment, her doctor would ask her what her questions were, and Saje would smile and say, "I don't know . . . nothing, really." She could tell her doctor found this surprising and would encourage her to ask anything, but she stayed small—which isn't her usual way of being, as she's often outspoken and can advocate for herself. Yet somewhere in the pregnancy journey, she bought into this idea that she didn't deserve to be pregnant.

Because Saje perceived herself as not ready for motherhood, there was a deep-seated belief that the world perceived her this way as well. When it was getting close to the time to announce her pregnancy, she kept putting it off. Even once she had announced it, she avoided the topic. And when she examined these feelings, she couldn't quite explain them but also wasn't able to stop feeling them. It wasn't that she feared she wouldn't love her son; it was the opposite—it was her Knowing of how much she would love him that terrified her. She was uncertain she was ready for that kind of selfless love, of allowing her heart to expand outside herself.

As her pregnancy progressed, Saje eventually came up with a plan for when she went into labor. She and Anthony took a hypnobirthing class. Hypnobirthing allows a woman's body to do what it is meant to do: have a baby in its own perfect way. The philosophy is against almost all interventions done in a typical hospital delivery room. For instance, most doctors will tell you it's time to push once you reach ten centimeters, but in hypnobirthing, they teach that you should not push until you feel the overwhelming urge to do so and that often, pushing isn't necessary at all—the baby will just make their way down the birth canal through the power of "surges" (contractions). Saje thought the class was a little extreme but wanted to attempt an all-natural birth. Our mom gave birth to all seven of her children without any pain-management interventions and regularly told us it wasn't painful; you just had to stay in the right frame of mind, one contraction at a time.

Fast-forward to the end of March 2019 as Saje's due date of April 6 approached. She started having Braxton Hicks (or light prelabor) contractions pretty frequently, and one morning, they started coming in a regular pattern —every four or five minutes like clockwork. She didn't tell anyone except Anthony, because she knew that even if this was the start of labor, it was very early and was nothing to sound the alarm about. Randomly, our mom sent Saje a text saying, "I can't stop thinking about you. Are you starting to feel labor coming on?" Saje told her about the contractions but was convinced this wasn't labor because there was absolutely nothing uncomfortable about them. The contractions stopped by the evening.

Our mom came to New York that day anyway to be with Saje until Julian arrived. She helped make their apartment more of a home for the arrival of their son and showered them with gifts, but more important, she spread her loving and mothering energy throughout their home, making Saje feel more ready to become a mother. Each day felt longer than the one before as they waited for any indication that true labor was starting, and every evening, they went for a walk with the unspoken hope that the activity would bring it on.

On April 4, Saje lay down on the couch, ready to resign for the evening and hope that labor would come the next day. But then she sat up abruptly and announced, "Something just popped!"

Our mom said, "This is it!"

She was right. A minute after that pop, it was clear that Saje's water had broken, and they set off for the hospital.

Delivering a baby is challenging no matter what the circumstances, but Saje's labor and delivery turned out to be one of the most harrowing and challenging days of her life. Although she'd had a completely healthy pregnancy without a single complication, she ended up having two different syndromes that came on during labor, causing her delivery to be extremely high risk. Her body essentially began to break down, and she was told by her doctors that without medical intervention, she likely would not survive her labor, and neither would her baby. Saje's organs were failing, and she risked having a seizure, which would cut off blood flow to the baby. Her body had become so swollen from retaining fluid that she could no longer see. She had to be treated with a drug that caused her to continuously vomit, not to mention that it just made her feel plain awful. Her labor had dragged on with extremely slow progress and increasing complications, so she eventually decided to ask for a C-section. But she was told she was not eligible for one because her blood had gotten so thin it would not clot, and she risked bleeding to death.

Saje received these words from the doctor as a call to surrender. She accepted that this day would be nothing like what she had envisioned, and it was not a time to fight but to accept and flow.

About twenty hours after her water initially broke, it was finally time to push. Saje pushed for more than two and a half hours until finally, a gray, slippery, limp Julian Wayne DeGrezia was born.

Julian was not placed on my chest as I had envisioned but instead rushed to a table, where a team of pediatricians worked on him. Although my eyes were virtually swollen shut at this point, I listened with every fiber of my being. When I heard them announce he was not breathing, I felt I could not breathe. My world froze as I waited and waited for some signal that he was making progress. Each second lasted an eternity. Finally, I started to hear soft whimpers from my little boy and could sense from the doctors' reactions that this was progress. Slowly, ever so slowly, those whimpers grew stronger, until I heard a cry that made my heart sing. In total, it was over fifteen minutes that the doctors worked with Julian until they were satisfied with his breathing and appearance. And after the most exhausting, frightening, and challenging twenty-three hours of my life, all I could think about for those fifteen minutes was somebody else.

This was the beginning of my understanding of what true, unconditional, divine love really is. When Julian was finally handed to me, I still could barely see, but what I felt was beyond imagination.

It was more than falling in love with him, more than my heart exploding; it was a Knowing. A Knowing that we were meant for each other. That all was in divine order and that I had just received the greatest gift of my lifetime. A Knowing that God's plan for me is far greater than what I had imagined, far greater than *me*.

As Saje writes this, she is almost a year into her parenting journey. After reflecting on who she was during her pregnancy, her labor experience, and this new life that she lives as a mother, it turns out that many of the fears she had during her pregnancy were not unreasonable. Her life is completely different: many of the freedoms she used to enjoy are no longer her reality, and she has had to make big adjustments. However, as it turns out, none of these things were anything to fear at all, because her life has been enriched in a way that she cannot put into words. She is not saying that it has all been rainbows and butterflies, because it certainly has not, and each stage of being a mother has brought its own set of challenges, but in this mix is a newer and deeper meaning to her life, not to mention a love like she has never known.

One day amid all of this, she went for a walk with Julian and listened to Dad's podcast. In it, he had a conversation with someone who was going through a difficult time in their life, and he recited the famous line from the Tao Te Ching, "There is no way to happiness; happiness is the way." Although this was a quote she'd heard a thousand times before, this time it resonated with her. There is no way to happiness—becoming a mom is not the way to happiness, nor is staying single and traveling the world. Instead, you bring the happiness to wherever you are in life. She brings the happiness to motherhood. She can sit in her apartment and choose to see it as a lonely prison, or she can choose to see it as the biggest blessing in her life to be able to spend this beautiful time raising her little love bug.

The choice is yours every single day. And this is not true just for parenting but for every situation. One job is not happier than another. Instead, you bring the happiness to your job, and then it becomes a happy job. Feeling good is feeling God. Like attracts like. You do not get in life what you want; you get in life what you are. When you want something, you must become a vibrational match to what it is that you are seeking, and being in a state of joy makes you a magnet for miracles.

In this new job as a parent, Saje likes to remind herself of the lines from Khalil Gibran our dad loved to recite. "Your children are not your children. They are the sons and daughters of life's longing for itself. Though they come through you but not from you, and though they are with you yet they belong not to you . . . "[1] These words are now a canvas in Julian's room, and she reads them often to remind herself as he grows that his life is his, and she is here to guide him when he seeks guidance, to care for him when he needs care, but most important, to love him, divinely and without conditions.

We have a sibling who has suffered from addiction, and Saje used to sit in judgment of our parents every time they picked up the pieces of her life and put it back together for her. Saje would proclaim that she would never "get better" unless they instituted some "tough" love. Whether this is true she does not know, but she no longer sits in judgment of this absolute need to love and care for their child. Saje sat in the car one day when the song "Time After Time" by Cyndi Lauper came on the radio, and as the song played, she felt a deep connection to the words that described a love in which no matter how many times someone may fall, you will be there to catch them again and again. She knew this was now true for her in regard to her son, Julian, for as long as she lived and beyond. And it was in that moment that she understood our parents' actions that she never could quite understand before. She now tries to muster that same divine and unconditional love she has for her son for our sister, for that is her birthright.

After Saje experienced such a harrowing labor, Serena knew she needed to get to New York and see Saje as soon as possible. She wanted to cook for her—to prepare meals to freeze for her so that she could be nourished while she began her journey as a first-time mom. So one week after Julian was born, Serena and her sixteen-week-old son, Forrest, boarded a plane to New York.

With tears in her eyes, Serena laid her baby next to her sister's. She was overcome with excitement at seeing the two boys meeting each other for the first time. Forrest and Julian locked arms, which we both captured in about two hundred photos in less than a minute, and all that had taken place in our lives that led to this moment of our sons' meeting was suddenly poignant. And this moment was one of pure joy.

It had been four years since our father died, yet when our babies met, Serena felt that Dad's presence was pervasive. Rarely a minute goes by in which a joke, a favorite restaurant, a memory, or something wonderful she wishes she could share about her children doesn't make her miss him. Yet she takes what she's learned, especially as a parent, and tries to remember how much joy and humor he brought to every single moment. She tries to be more like him. Every memory of our father reminds her to choose love, to have love, because he lived that more than anyone she has ever known.

ALL THE WISDOM OF THE UNIVERSE

We arrive in this world alone, and we leave alone. Our dad always said he had a coat in his closet with the pockets cut out to remind him that we take nothing with us, nothing but our own experiences, our own growth, and the love we shared along the way. We encounter situations and individuals that challenge our souls to grow, expand, and evolve. Without this difficult time in our lives, perhaps we would never have come to know and love ourselves the way we do now. And isn't that what it's all about anyway? Learning to love who we are?

Our dad used to say you can never be lonely if you like the person you're alone with. Prior to his death, Serena liked certain things about herself. She liked that she was young and grew up wealthy and pretty. Saje concerned herself with the opinions of others and was hyperfocused on the logical or what she could prove. During the difficult years that followed Dad's death, we began to realize that none of that was important. More than that, we realized that none of those things were even real.

The loss of our dad is pervasive. We imagine it is that way for anyone who loses a parent that is larger than life, as our dad was for us. Rarely a minute goes by in which something doesn't trigger a thought about him . . .

Serena sees a BMW driving in front of her and remembers the time Dad bought a BMW for Mom, her first car of her own after driving a minivan for years. Ten years old at the time, Serena asked Dad what BMW meant. He told her it stood for "bowel movement for Wayne." For months, she repeated that explanation to our friends' parents, knowing it made adults laugh but not understanding quite why.

Saje checks her mailbox and recalls the excitement of seeing our dad's scratchy handwriting in purple ink on an envelope. Our dad regularly sent us cards, often for no reason at all, and sometimes with a gift inside. Receiving those letters is something Saje will always cherish.

Serena has dinner at an Indian restaurant and thinks about the time she and her family ate at an Indian place in Las Vegas together and how it was that one meal that triggered her love for Indian food, a fondness she and Dad shared, and how many countless nights on Maui they would order Indian takeout, much to the chagrin of our siblings who didn't share their passion.

Saje's iPad starts to malfunction, and it reminds her of the many, many phone calls during which she had to walk our dad through how to upgrade his phone, download a necessary app, or call someone via FaceTime. Or the time she set up an Apple TV for him and wrote out extensive step-by-step directions for how to search for a movie title. His irritation at the "complication" of technology always made us laugh.

When Serena makes coffee in the morning, she remembers how Dad, in the last years of his life, started doing coffee enemas and would tell all of us siblings that we were drinking coffee the wrong way, that "the best part of waking up was Folger's in your butt." Or that he was starting a chain of coffeehouses and calling it Starbutts.

Saje takes a yoga class and thinks back to the many classes she took with Dad and how he would grab her toe when the instructor wasn't looking so she'd lose her balance. He loved to act "annoyed" at the fact that he had been practicing yoga for months, and she went to her first class with him and could already do a camel pose!

When Serena flosses her teeth, she thinks of the countless—and she means *countless*—times our dad chased her with his used piece of floss, laughing and shrieking that she could sell it on eBay and someone would pay big bucks for it.

Saje often thinks about how Dad would walk into the living room and see her relaxing or taking it easy and say, "Don't worry, just stay relaxing there. I'm in my seventies, but I'll just continue working so that you can all have a nice life and relax whenever you want to. Don't worry about me. I'll be fine."

Anytime Saje hears the song "The Twist" by Chubby Checker, she's immediately reminded of our dad's dorky dance moves, with his tongue sticking out the side of his mouth. He loved to break into dance anytime a favorite oldie of his came on.

There isn't a part of any day in which we are not reminded of something he said or did, not a single part. Now that we are parents, we do our best to remember how much joy and humor Dad brought to every single situation and try to emulate that in our own households. We are incredibly grateful our dad was our dad and that we were able to have the time we did with him, watching a master at work—a master of love. He wanted us to always come from a place of love, even with the most difficult people or circumstances. He lived that more than anyone else we have ever known. That really would be his greatest lesson to us all: to choose love, have love, be love.

A Way of Knowing

Returning to love, kindness, and receptivity.

Many of the things we perceive as making us happy are completely subjective and therefore irrelevant, and the truth behind it all is that no "thing" makes us happy. We choose happiness. Being in a state of joy is paramount to attracting the life you desire. Of course, there are times that other feelings come up, and joy just seems impossible. What to do in these times? Feel the feeling, forgive the feeling, and attempt to shift your energy closer to joy, one emotional step at a time. Maybe this means going for a walk or taking a bath to stimulate the shift. Maybe it means nourishing your body with a healthy homemade meal or treating it to a delicious dessert. Whatever you have to do to get in alignment with joy.

There's often a perception that happiness is always somewhere else, somewhere down the road—ten pounds or ten thousand dollars away. But the reality is that happiness and joy are always available to us. They're just a thought away, because happiness is a mindset or a journey, not a destination. Sometimes we like to replace the word *happiness* with *purpose* or *meaning*, as we feel that in many ways, they are interchangeable.

People often ask, "What if I'm not living my purpose?" or "How do I find my purpose?" The answer is similar to our explanation about happiness. Your purpose is not a destination; it is a lifelong journey that will take you many, many places, and it will shift and take on newer and different meanings as you gain wisdom through aging. The key is to find meaning and purpose in each thing you do instead of spending time searching for your one purpose.

Right now, one of our biggest purposes is to be mothers to our children, and each day, we find meaning in this. There are countless dos and don'ts in motherhood, but as long as our actions are coming from love and we are modeling and teaching love to our children, we are fulfilling our mothering purpose, our dharma. We have our parents to thank for spending their lifetimes teaching us exactly that.

For Saje, it took giving birth to her son Julian, in all its complicated beauty, to awaken the divine love that exists within her. Prior to this, she went through life feeling amazed not nearly often enough, but today, even the simplest things excite her soul. She feels connected to everyone around her in a way she can't quite explain. Everything moves her, and getting "the chills" is a daily occurrence. The divine love within her that now exists with a loud presence exists within us all, and it most certainly does not take a child to awaken it.

As we bring this book to a close, we challenge you to contemplate your own death. It can feel odd or even incomprehensible to do so, as our egos resist this idea wholeheartedly. Freud observed that the idea of our death is unimaginable, so we simply deny it and live our lives as if we aren't going to die because of the terror our own death instills. The fear of death originates in its finality, but if you have embraced the notion that we are infinite and eternal beings, you know that this fear is founded in falsehood. And as you are able to contemplate your death more and more, you can come to a place in which you embrace the idea of your return ticket home.

With everything that we have experienced since losing our dad, we now go through life with the *Knowing* that we are eternal and infinite beings, and therefore, death is nothing to fear at all. Whether you live with this knowing or not, the ultimate truth of it does not change, which is why we challenge you to embrace and allow this to be the catalyst to living a life of more love, more service, and more compassion. Embrace the idea that death is the ultimate plunge into divine love. Live your life with the awareness that your time in this earth suit is limited, and let that be the catalyst to bringing more and more divine love into your life.

ACKNOWLEDGMENTS

First and foremost, we must acknowledge our parents, for we simply would not be who we are today without them, and their guidance has been what has allowed us to get to a place of recognizing that we all have an inner Knowing. Mom, you are the embodiment of what it means to be a mother. You have never offered anything to your children that is not based in love, and you have never wavered, not even once, from only teaching love as well. We love you. Dad, we reconnected to so much of your work in writing this book, and we know you had a hand in it, every step of the way. We miss you and the way it used to be, but we have come to know that you are still here, still being our dad, helping align all the pieces so we continue to get not just green lights but endless signs and messages from you as well. When we are reunited again, we will know why it had to be this way, but we'd like to think we are starting to have a clue here and now. Forever, Dad, we love you.

This book simply would not have been possible without the work of Alice Peck, our writer, editor, support, guide, and friend, who kept us on track, reminded us that we had a story to tell, and from day one of working together made us feel our words were deeply meaningful. Alice, you took our scattered notes and stories and transformed them into what we have today. From the deepest part of both of us, thank you!

To Gabby Bernstein, thank you for introducing us to Michele and for offering your guiding voice whenever we asked. Michele, you are a powerhouse, and you saw in us what we had not yet seen in ourselves. You helped us see the bigger picture of what our stories could become, and you reminded us time and again that this book had value. You are the rock-star agent we needed! We are so grateful for you and for introducing us to Alice!

We would like to thank everyone at Sounds True publishing, especially Diana Ventimiglia, who believed in us and this project before we even knew what we were doing!

We would like to thank all of our siblings, our siblings-in-law (bonus family members), our entire twenty-five-plus-person immediate family that never wavered in their support of our work! We really have the greatest family of all time, and we love you all beyond heaven and earth!

Serena would like to thank her closest friends, Lauren and Natalie. The two of you define what true friendship (going on twenty-plus years, OMG) looks like, and whatever I did to deserve you two by my side, thank you! I would also like to thank Avianna Castro for being the lighthouse for Matt and me during all of our trying times and constantly reminding me to stop playing small. Sarah-Renee for regularly reaching out with signs and messages from the other side and Karen Noe for first bringing us into contact with our dad after he passed and opening up many opportunities for us along the way.

Thank you to Dr. Marla Reis, who has continued to keep me in check and remind me of my own strengths and gifts, even when I didn't see them at all. Mason, there are no words to describe what you have given me. You taught me so much in the nine years I had you in my life in the physical realm and continue to from "the other room," and I am forever your student. I love you, my sweet friend. I am so grateful to have shared the time we had and continue to have. Last, I couldn't have done any of this without the love and support from my better half, Matt. You are the greatest father to our three children and Mason, and I have always, always felt how much you believe in me. Thank you for Mason and our babies, Sailor, Windsor, and Forrest; thank you for being so patient; thank you for loving me.

Saje would like to thank her closest friends, who keep her laughing and also grounded all at once—you know who you are! My incredible husband, Anthony, whose patience knows no end and whose love for our family is inspiring. Thank you for supporting my work with this book and for believing in me. I would also like to thank Karen Noe, Avianna Castro, and Sarah-Renee for being guiding lights to the Divine since our dad left the physical plane. Lastly, to my incredible son, Julian, for knowing I needed you before I did. You've opened my heart and given my life a divinely deeper meaning just by simply being you—I love you with everything I am. Your arrival in my life is what gave me the nudge I needed to get this book finished.

NOTES

INTRODUCTION:
RETURNING TO THE KNOWING

1. Christian Nestell Bovee, "The Apocryphal Twain: 'Kindness Is a Language the Deaf Can Hear,'" Center for Mark Twain Studies, marktwainstudies .com/apocryphaltwainoptimism/.

2. "What Life Means to Einstein," Saturday Evening Post, saturdayeveningpost.com/wp-content/uploads /satevepost/what_life_means_to_einstein.pdf.

3. Douglas K. DeVorss in Baird Thomas Spalding's *Life and Teaching of the Masters of the Far East* (Camarillo, CA: DeVorss, 1996).

CHAPTER 1
WHAT IS THIS TEACHING ME?

1. Helen Schucman, *A Course in Miracles* (Omaha, NE: Course in Miracles Society, 1976), Workbook, Lesson 34.

2. Emily Dickinson, *The Complete Poems*, ed. Thomas H. Johnson (Boston: Little, Brown, 1960), 395.

3. C. G. Jung, *The Collected Works of C.G. Jung: Complete Digital Edition* (Princeton, NJ: Princeton University Press, 2014).

4. Victor E. Frankl, *Man's Search for Meaning* (Boston: Beacon Press, 2006), 112.

5. Schucman, *A Course in Miracles*, 378.

CHAPTER 2
PARENTED IN PURE LOVE

1. **enthusiasm (n.)** c. 1600, from Middle French *enthousiasme* (16c.) and directly from Late Latin *enthousiasmus*, from Greek *enthousiasmos* "divine inspiration, enthusiasm (produced by certain kinds of music, etc.)," from *enthousiazein* "be inspired or possessed by a god, be rapt, be in ecstasy," from *entheos* "divinely inspired, possessed by a god," from *en* "in" (see **en-** (2)) + *theos* "god" (from PIE root ***dhes-**, forming words for religious concepts). From etymonline.com/word/enthusiasm.

2. Viktor Emil Frankl, *Man's Search for Meaning* (Boston: Beacon Press, 2006), 89.

3. Luke 23:34 (King James Version).

CHAPTER 3
THE MIND FORGETS BUT
THE SOUL REMEMBERS

1. Wayne W. Dyer, *Change Your Thoughts, Change Your Life: Living the Wisdom of the Tao* (Carlsbad, CA: Hay House, Incorporated, 2007), 4.

2. Wayne W. Dyer, *I Can See Clearly Now* (Carlsbad, CA: Hay House, Incorporated, 2014), 149.

CHAPTER 4
FROM NO WHERE TO NOW HERE

1. Acts 9:3–9 (New Revised Standard Version).

CHAPTER 5
STARS IN DAYLIGHT

1. Herman Melville, *Moby Dick* (United Kingdom: St. Botolph Society, 1892), 287.

2. Sebcam, "Law of Attraction Quote of the Day," Steemit, steemit.com/art/@sebcam/law-of-attraction -quote-of-the-day-art-of-being-who-you-really-are. Adapted from a speech Esther Hicks gave in Ashland, Oregon, on July 20, 2002.

CHAPTER 6
CHOOSING SOONER

1. Roy and Jane Nichols, "Funerals: A Time for Grief and Growth," in *Death: The Final Stage of Growth*, ed. Elisabeth Kübler-Ross (Englewood Cliffs, NJ: Prentice-Hall, 1975), 96.

CHAPTER 7
TAKE YOUR SHOES OFF

1. Herman Melville, *Complete Works of Herman Melville (Illustrated)* (East Sussex, UK: Delphi Classics, 2013), Bk XIV, ch.1.

2. Wayne W. Dyer, *Getting in the Gap* (Carlsbad, CA: Hay House, Incorporated, 2002), 71.

3. Elizabeth Barrett Browning, *The Poetical Works of Elizabeth Barrett Browning: With Two Prose Essays*, 10th Ed., Vol. 5 (United Kingdom: Smith, Elder & Co., 1873), 308.

4. Wayne Dyer's interpretation of a Rumi poem, from Wayne W. Dyer, *I Can See Clearly Now*, page 351.

5. Carlos Castaneda, *Power of Silence* (New York: Atria Books, 2013), 147.

6. Herman Melville, *Pierre, or, The Ambiguities* (New York: Harper & Brothers, 1852), 192.

7. Browning, *The Poetical Works of Elizabeth Barrett Browning*, 304.

CHAPTER 8
THE GEOMETRY OF FORGIVENESS

1. Prayer of Saint Francis: This work is in the public domain in the United States because it was legally published within the United States between 1923 and 1977 (inclusive) without a copyright notice.

CHAPTER 9
YIELDING TO THE SIGNS

1. Daniel Ladinsky, *The Subject Tonight Is Love: 60 Wild and Sweet Poems of Hafiz* (London: Penguin Compass, 2003), 13.

2. See note for chapter 8.

CHAPTER 10
THE PATH OF LEAST RESISTANCE

1. Herman Melville, *Moby Dick*, 287.

2. Anne Lamott, *Crooked Little Heart: A Novel* (New York: Knopf Doubleday Publishing Group, 2011), 236.

3. "The *Oprah Winfrey Show* Finale," Oprah.com, oprah.com/oprahshow/the-oprah-winfrey-show-finale_1.

4. "Maya Angelou > Quotes > Quotable Quote," Goodreads, goodreads.com/quotes/7532767-forgive-yourself-for-not-knowing-what-you-didn-t-know-before.

CHAPTER 11
ESPECIALLY LOVE

1. Kahlil Gibran, "On Children," Poets.org, poets.org /poem/children-1.

ABOUT THE AUTHORS

Saje Dyer grew up in Boca Raton, Florida, and moved to New York, where she graduated from NYU with a master's degree in psychology. Her first book was a children's book titled *Good-bye, Bumps! Talking to What's Bugging You*, which tells the true story of how she was able to heal herself as a child through the power of the mind. Saje often traveled with her Dad, Dr. Wayne Dyer, to tell the story to his audiences, and she recently appeared on his PBS special. Saje is a mother to her little boy, Julian, and she enjoys traveling, learning, and spending time with loved ones. Saje is the youngest of eight children, so family is and always has been an important part of her life.

Serena Dyer Pisoni is the coauthor of *Don't Die With Your Music Still In You*, which she wrote with her father, Dr. Wayne Dyer. Serena attended the University of Miami, where she received bachelor's and master's degrees, and resides in South Florida with her husband and three children.

ABOUT SOUNDS TRUE

Sounds True is a multimedia publisher whose mission is to inspire and support personal transformation and spiritual awakening. Founded in 1985 and located in Boulder, Colorado, we work with many of the leading spiritual teachers, thinkers, healers, and visionary artists of our time. We strive with every title to preserve the essential "living wisdom" of the author or artist. It is our goal to create products that not only provide information to a reader or listener but also embody the quality of a wisdom transmission.

For those seeking genuine transformation, Sounds True is your trusted partner. At SoundsTrue.com you will find a wealth of free resources to support your journey, including exclusive weekly audio interviews, free downloads, interactive learning tools, and other special savings on all our titles.

To learn more, please visit SoundsTrue.com/freegifts or call us toll-free at 800.333.9185.